RIDING

TO MUSIC

RIDING TO MUSIC

Music and Choreography for the
Individual Kur, Pas de Deux,
and the Classical Quadrille

WERNER STORL

Illustrations by

ULRICK SCHRAMM

Translated from the German by

SANDRA L. NEWKIRK

Breakthrough
PUBLICATIONS

For information address:

Breakthrough Publications, Inc.
Millwood, New York 10546

International Standard Book Number: 0-914327-17-8
Library of Congress Catalog Card Number: 86-64061
Book design by Jacques Chazaud

Manufactured in the United States of America

1 2 3 4 5 6 7 8 9 0

Contents

Foreword

Riding to music is an art that is becoming more and more important on the international horse scene. With the increasing interest in Kur and Quadrille competition, riders today are finding it necessary to widen the horizons of their standard repertoires to be able to choreograph a ballet-like ride.

In fact, history shows a centuries-old tradition of riding to music that leads from the ancient days of Xenophon through the Middle Ages, the Renaissance, and the Baroque era to the sporting life of today with its World Cup for Dressage and the new wave of Quadrille competition. Tournements, trionfis, carrousels, and horse ballets—the classical traditions as preserved in Vienna, Saumur, and Andalusia—are clearly evident in the cultural stream that has flowed down through history to influence today's and future generations of riders.

Classical riding, in combination with one of the "beautiful arts," music, leads to another art—ballet on horseback. Heritage obliges, requiring efforts to master the skills necessary to perform these ballets.

Werner Storl, the author of *Riding to Music*, shares here his approach to the practice of this art, based on his years of experience. He introduces us to the historical roots of riding to music and shows us how to incorporate these traditions into our rides. He offers a pioneering work for which we must give thanks.

I personally wish this book, as a guide and introduction, a lot of success.

Gabriela Grillo
Mülheim-Ruhr, Germany

Preface

The individual and pairs kur ridden to music selected by the riders is enjoying increasing popularity. Just as happily, the quadrille is also experiencing a renaissance, and competitions are being held which are exclusively for the quadrille.

Over and over, however, I've observed a certain helplessness at these competitions in the musical presentation. This uncertainty in the choice and presentation of suitable musical accompaniment has encouraged me to write this book.

My explorations are mostly in the area of the quadrille, and I have devoted an entire section of the book to the quadrille competition. Nevertheless, the ideas and suggestions discussed are equally applicable for the individual kur, pas de deux, and other rides to music.

I have scrutinized every piece of music I've heard in the past few years for its suitability for the quadrille. Thus the reader will find here more than 170 works listed, most of which are also annotated with metronome count and playing time. As many works listed, such as symphonies and ballet works, are composed of several sections, there is a total of 250 examples of music to ride to.

This book has been made possible through my many years of practical work with the quadrille, and I would like to express my special thanks to all those riders who have worked with me these past years on this wonderful task. Most especially, I thank the riders of my "Rossini Quadrille" from the riding club at Bredenbecker Teich in Hamburg.

Many, many thanks to Dr. Lachmann, initiator of the annual quadrille championships at the riding club in Wohldorf, as well as to the Hamburg State Association that adopted the idea of a quadrille competition and gave it life by establishing the special Quadrille Competition Task Force and promoting the annual quadrille show in the Exhibitors' Halls in Hamburg. The experiences of working with the Task Force and the competitions themselves have formed the basis for this book.

Further thanks to my riding comrade of many years, Director Hans-Joachim Reincke, who kindly edited this manuscript.

Especial thanks to my wife who, for years, has patiently put up with my sitting at the record player with stopwatch and pencil in hand.

I also wish to thank Paul Parey Publishers and their staff for their understanding and for the publishing of these ideas.

Lastly, I wish to thank the horses themselves who made this work with all its pinnacles and disappointments possible in the first place.

Tangstedt
January, 1986   Werner Storl

PART I

DEVELOPMENT OF THE QUADRILLE AND FUNDAMENTALS OF MUSIC

CHAPTER ONE

A Short History of the Quadrille

The riding quadrille developed from the dance of the same name, an elegant configuration of danced patterns that originated in France. It was a kind of square dance, usually done in five rounds to duple or triple time. This quadrille formed an integral part of the curriculum at European schools of dance well into the 1940s. At every ball it was either the ceremonious opening or crowned the high point of the evening. Music written especially for the quadrille carried the rhythm of the figures. A well-known example of this genre, used to open many such stately occasions, is the *Fledermaus Quadrille* from the operetta of the same name by Johann Strauss.

The quadrille with its richness of varied figures in which the dancers merge into groups and then disperse into smaller units gave rise early in its history to the ridden quadrille, which in turn was to become the cornerstone for all ceremonial occasions within the classical school of riding. At Italian courts, so-called horse ballets were held, and by as early as the middle of the seventeenth century, Kaiser Leopold I of Austria had introduced these spectacular equestrian demonstrations to Vienna. There, on January 24, 1667, an opulent equestrian festival took place in honor of the Kaiser's marriage to the Spanish Infanta, Margaretha Theresia. These grandiose equestrian demonstrations became known as the "carousel."

Originally riding contests with saber and lance, the carousel comprised a rich and varied program. A contemporary reports:

The carousel began with spearing the ring, followed by exercises with short lances. Next the riders charged with swords drawn, beheading wooden figures of Turkish soldiers with a single stroke. Slicing apples suspended from strings in two with a curved saber while riding at a full gallop was even more difficult, requiring a good eye and extraordinary skill. The quadrille to the accompaniment of military music formed the transition between these games. The scene then changed and two groups of four riders each charged in mock battle, attempting to knock one another out of the saddle. Finally, the entire cavalcade divided itself into two parties, each consisting of twelve knights with their pages riding one intricate evolution after another. These groups of twelve would merge, then quickly form fronts of twelve, six, and four riders abreast. As a final demonstration of the tractability and skillfulness of their mounts, the knights then executed a kind of dance in perfect time with the music.[1]

Another extensive report on such a carousel can be found in the "Newsletter for Horse Lovers," volume 24, from the year 1826.[2] This particular carousel was held by Reichsgraf von Hohberg on May 20, 1808 at Castle Forstenburg in the Sudeten Mountains. According to this report, the "quadrille" consisted of a group of four riders in matching, elegant dress. One by one, under the watchful eye of the head judge, they were tested in the various tournament games such as described in the earlier report from Vienna. Three of the four quadrilles then took part in a single carousel. It would seem from this that today's pas de quatre is probably one of the earliest forms of the ridden quadrille.

The crowned heads and nobility from all over Europe issued invitations to one another to attend such carousels at their courts. And in 1735, following the completion of the famous Riding Hall of the Spanish Riding School, Vienna became the hub of equestrian gala performances. During this period of glorious performances, many musical works, usually pieces for brass, were composed for these festivals. From Beethoven's pen, for example, we have the *Music for a Horse Ballet*.

In 1894 the last grand carousel in Vienna took place, in which 125 riders, 14 coaches, and 4 pieces of artillery participated, and snow-white Lippizaners danced to the music.[3] Still today the grand school quadrille of the Spanish Riding School, which till the end of World War I was shown only to invited guests of the imperial house, is among the loveliest of equestrian experiences (see figure 1). The music used for these gala performances is by Strauss, Mozart, Boccherini, Bizet, and Chopin.

---

1. Federal Ministry for Agriculture and Forestry, ed., *The Spanish Riding School in Vienna* (West Germany, 1965).

2. "Newsletter for Horse Lovers," (Dortmund, West Germany: Bibliophile Pocketbooks, Harenburg Communications, 1977).

3. Federal Ministry for Agriculture and Forestry, ed., *The Spanish Riding School in Vienna* (West Germany, 1965).

Figure 1

CHI Berlin 1978. The grand school quadrille of the Spanish Riding School in Vienna. The eight white stallions are the embodiment of living baroque performing to music of the classical era. (Photo: W. Menzendorf)

Figure 2

The Cadre Noir from the French Cavalry School in Saumur. Elegance and expressiveness in the highest degree of collection. (Photo: W. Menzendorf)

In addition to the Spanish Riding School, two other famous institutions for classical riding were established: The French Riding Academy at Saumur with its famous "Cadre Noir," and, in Germany, the Military Riding Institute of Hanover, later known as the Hanover Cavalry School. The French academy, in existence since 1814, is the officers' training institute for the French army. The Cadre Noir, its school quadrille, wears black uniforms with gold braid and is mounted, for the most part, on English Thoroughbreds (figure 2).

The Italians, too, had a school quadrille: the "Carosello dei Carabinier." Sabers drawn, in blue uniforms and mounted on white horses galloping towards one another in mock battle, they thrilled the public.

The Royal Canadian Mounted Police maintains a quadrille of thirty-two horses. In scarlet coats and carrying traditional lances, this troupe has made public appearances since 1904. This quadrille, which performs very large and intricate figures, gives over 100 performances per year throughout the world.

In Germany each year a knowledgeable and enthusiastic equestrian public gathers each year at the State Stud in Celle to see the famous stallion quadrille. These performances are always sold out weeks in advance.

A local riding club in northern Germany, the Hurden Riding Club, maintains a quadrille of twenty horses, the "Blue Riders." This troupe, named for their light blue coats, has found public acclaim far beyond their local community. Steppingstones in their success have included performances in the famous Deutschlandhalle in Berlin, the Westfalenhalle in Dortmund, and the City Hall in the city of Bremen.

The driving quadrilles of the Swiss Army's harnessed artillery, made up of coaches of six with the driver astride, and its driving quadrilles with coachs of four shown often at equestrian events, round out this picture of the quadrille tradition.

We cannot discuss the development of the quadrille in Germany without mentioning the name Oscar Fritz. By 1925, he had found great acclaim in and around Berlin and was generally considered to be a true master of the art of the quadrille.

In 1939 a performance of the Cadre Noir from Saumur held at the international horse show in the Deutschlandhalle in Berlin under the leadership of Cadet Lessage made such an impression on the German officers that they decided to create a German school quadrille. One of the era's most brilliant riders, Felix Bürkner was chosen for this task (figure 3). In that year, Bürkner took over the Cavalry School in Hanover. This was later moved to Potsdam-Krampnitz and renamed the Army School of Riding and Driving.

Promoted to colonel and named commander of the school, Bürkner trained a twelve-horse quadrille through painstaking and patient work in

Figure 3
International riding and driving show in the Deutschlandhalle in Berlin, 1939. A historical photo of the Cadre Noir. It was this performance that inspired the creation of the German School Quadrille under the leadership of Felix Bürkner. (Photo: W. Menzendorf)

Figure 4
A racy jumping quadrille. The St. Hubertus Riding Club in Obrighoven/Niederrhein, Germany. (Photo: W. Menzendorf)

the individual movements through the Fourth Level. Among the trainers assigned to the school were Willi Schultheis, Fritz Thiedemann, Walter Günther, and "Ede" Fink.[4]

Bürkner built his quadrille on the basis of classical dressage and placed great emphasis on using music as it was originally written. He measured the figures of his quadrille exactly in seconds and meters. His music consultant, an expert named Witeschnik who later became Professor of Music in Vienna, designed a finely turned score from classical sources for this quadrille.

During the years of its existence, from 1940–1943, this German School Quadrille became one of the equestrian world's most stirring experiences. Unfortunately Bürkner's retirement in 1943 brought to an end this high point of the quadrille tradition in Germany.

At the closing ceremonies of the 1972 Olympics in Munich, the Bürkner quadrille was revived. It was later repeated at several international horse shows throughout Europe. With the help of twelve of Germany's best dressage riders, Albert Stecken, Walter Günther, and Willi Schultheis created this spectacular olympic quadrille patterned closely on its original. The participating riders included Dr. Reiner Klimke, Ilsebill Becher, Willi Schultheis, Inge Theodorescu, Walter Günther, Gabriela Grillo, Harry Boldt, and Eva-Marie Pracht.

This return performance of Bürkner's School Quadrille reawakened the art of the quadrille in Germany, at the same time establishing guideposts and performance criteria for the future.

Those of us today who wish to practice this art should not lose sight of the monumental accomplishments of these past masters.

DEVELOPMENTS SINCE 1945

In the years following the war, Dr. h. c. Gustav Rau gave new impetus to riding in Germany. Following World War I, he had created the system of local riding clubs in Germany. Now, after World War II, he brought these back to life and helped in their reorganization.

In these years, an understandable reaction against everything that had a military or authoritarian character had spread, even to the sport of riding. No one wanted to hear the echoes of the barracks yard drill anymore.

Young riders at this time focused more on individual performance in dressage, jumping, and cross-country. Thanks to Germany's "Economic Miracle" of the sixties and seventies, many riders were able and prepared to pay well for horses, which they then, of course, wanted to show. Individual performance tests seemed the only appropriate avenue.

---

4. E. Fink was my riding instructor in Hamburg from 1956 to 1958. I was able to learn much from him. He died on New Year's Eve, 1978, while in the stable among his beloved horses.

But thanks to instructors who revived the musical rides in celebration of New Year's and Fasching,* young riders in Germany were introduced to the joys of riding in groups to music. Even the most diehard individualist could see that these formations were possible only by practicing as a group under the direction of an instructor.

Thus it was that the musical ride experienced a renaissance in Germany, Today there is hardly a riding club that does not offer a musical ride or perform a special quadrille for Christmas or other occasions. Indeed, the musical ride has become a regular offering in the programs of most riding clubs, especially in the winter.

GLIMPSING THE FUTURE

Influenced by visits to the Spanish Riding School in Vienna or by performances of these famous school quadrilles on television, many a rider has felt a desire to take part in a more structured musical ride, to take part in a true quadrille. In the last few years we have seen more and more high-level dressage tests being offered as a musical freestyle (kur) at horse shows. Some riding clubs are even holding entire competitions focused on the quadrille. These have been gaining quite a lot in popularity and have been accorded regional television coverage in Germany. As yet, no rules for these competitions have been established by the LPO** except the existing rules of general application to dressage competitions. Guidelines, however, have been developed locally and successfully implemented. At the riding club in Hamburg, for example, a Quadrille Competition Task Force, staffed by the club's officers, quadrille directors, and recognized judges, has been working for several years to develop guidelines and scoring sheets. It is particularly pleasing to note that a team of judges is working intensively on this competition prototype and is already successfully judging such competitions.

The individual kur to music, which has long suffered under benevolent neglect, was given new momentum with the creation of the World Cup for Dressage, which was held for the first time in the spring of 1986 in the Netherlands. For this competition, one required test at the Grand Prix level and one kur program were ridden, with the kur being given 50 percent greater value in the overall score. Thus from a mere "show number" used to entertain the audience during the breaks at competitions, this true capstone of classical riding, the dancing horse, the musical kur, has finally come into its own.

Translator's Note: Fasching or Karneval is a period of general revelry that comes just before Lent. It is a time of merry-making and costume balls.

**Translator's Note:* The LPO (Leistungprufungsordung) is the German equivalent to the AHSA rule book.

CHAPTER TWO

From Musical Ride
to Quadrille

In introducing this discussion of the quadrille and kur, let me emphasize that we are not talking about a musical ride in which a group rides to the tune of the radio blasting the latest hits interspersed with traffic reports. To qualify as a quadrille, three elements are interwoven:

1. *Riding Style:* A quadrille is ridden based on internationally recognized dressage standards and guidelines. These focus on the seat and influence of the rider and the suppleness, impulsion, and, where appropriate, collection of the horse. The difficulty of the specific figures should be geared to the recognized test levels, which can range from Training through Fourth Level. The rider's seat and influence on the horse should reflect at least the level being ridden.

2. *Aesthetics:* By this I mean how well the horses match, the quality of the group's turnout, the level of difficulty of the various figures and how well they are choreographed, and, finally, the way in which the figures are woven into the fabric of the music.

3. *Music:* A major element of the quadrille is the music to which it is set, which establishes the entire atmosphere for the performance.

It is from these three elements that the classical quadrille is created. This book has been written largely as an aid to finding and arranging the music for such a quadrille.

SELECTION OF HORSES
AND RIDERS

The Horses

Let's start with the assumption that the ideal quadrille for the small to middle-sized club would consist of eight horses. Eight willing school horses that have basic training will constitute a sufficient group through First Level work. Working in the same school and living in the same barn, they should be used to one another and able to tolerate working together in close quarters. It is of the utmost importance that the horses tolerate one another; horses that kick or bite are not suitable. When in doubt, it is preferable to use a reliable mount which is a somewhat dull mover to the horse with lots of impulsion who gets nervous at the wrong moment. At the Training Level*, under inexperienced riders, horses could even be ridden in side reins.

The Riders

I am assuming that the reader has some experience evaluating riders. Still, I'd like to highlight some important specifics. A quadrille is as good as its weakest rider. Also, riders who have trouble following orders, who aren't "team players," who can't pay attention, or who are constant debaters and notorious know-it-alls will always be a problem in forming a quadrille team. To create something of quality, the participating riders must be selected with care.

One basic assumption is that to ride a First Level quadrille, the riders should be competent at that level and that riders selected for upper level quadrilles should have competed at these levels as well. Especially in the quadrille, one can often see a great discrepancy between what should be and the various riders' actual capabilities. There are more than just a few riders who feel that the mere possession of a derby or top hat qualifies them to ride at the higher levels.

Waldemar Seunig, a revered officer and great humanitarian, made the following observation:

> True readiness for the double bridle—both among horses and riders—is found much less frequently than is generally believed. The double bridle should be seen as well-earned documentation that, at a minimum, one has completed one's "apprenticeship" as a rider.[5]

Translator's Note: Training Level per se does not exist in Germany; however, it serves as a valid equivalent in this context for the "E" Level tests designed for novice riders.

5. Waldemar Seunig, *From Corral to Capriole* (Frankfurt, West Germany: Wolfgang Kruger, 1980).

When selection of horses and riders is complete, planning for the quadrille figures can proceed. Here the basic rule of thumb is: simple figures that are well executed are far preferable to pushing the limits of the group's capability.

PLANNING
LENGTH AND FIGURES

The Length
A quadrille's performance should run between ten and fifteen minutes. Anything longer than this would tire the audience. I find twelve minutes to be ideal.

The Figures
It goes without saying that the ability level of the horses and riders involved will determine the limits of difficulty for the figures to be used. If the quadrille is to be shown in competition, then the existing guidelines for that particular competition must be adhered to.

CHOOSING THE MUSIC

Before we consider the actual planning of the quadrille, let's focus first on our actual topic—the music for the quadrille. As I've said previously, don't underestimate the importance of the music, for it is the music that unites the riders, the horses, and the audience. From the very first beat it determines the atmosphere of the whole.

If the quadrille is to be ridden for a particular occasion, the music chosen should highlight this. Thus, a quadrille performed for New Year's could be done to the music of Johann Strauss*. For a Fasching quadrille, music by Offenbach, jazz, and ragtime come to mind. Music by Mozart, Beethoven, and Handel would befit more formal occasions.

The music should also be appropriate to the level of the quadrille being ridden. For example, a first quadrille attempt based on Training Level figures and with riders who don't yet sit quite in harmony with the horse shouldn't be ridden to a symphony by Beethoven.

The level of the quadrille and the music chosen should also be appropriate for the audience, the setting of the performance (i.e., the arena), and the staging or decorations (such as flags and flowers). A Fourth Level quadrille ridden in the Deutschlandhalle in Berlin will inspire its audience with a different kind of music than that chosen for the first local attempt

---

Translator's Note: The music of Johann Strauss is traditional New Year's fare in Austria and Germany.

at a Training Level quadrille.

In addition to the equestrian basics, a successful quadrille requires a good measure of feel, imagination, and inspiration. From all this we can conclude that to qualify as a good quadrille director, one must be a felicitous mixture of riding teacher, musician, choreographer, and pyschologist.

In planning for the quadrille, we shouldn't lose sight of the fact that the classical quadrille was originally a gallant, courtly dance. As the ballet, too, is music to which a rich variety of harmonious figures is danced, it is perhaps fitting that this serve as our prototype or vision. Even if this analogy seems a bit exaggerated to some, I see the quadrille as a ballet for horses patterned after the famous quadrille of the Spanish Riding School and the legendary one created at the Hanover Cavalry School.

Having selected horses and riders and having established the level of difficulty to be performed, we can now begin to look for an appropriate musical selection. This can proceed in two ways:

1. We can first develop the figures and movements and then find suitable music. This, however, is not particularly recommended. Done this way, music usually has to be frequently interrupted and changed.

2. We'll first find a fitting piece of music, suitable for what we want in the way of atmosphere and length. Then we'll build the equestrian work into the music. This method might take more time and planning, but it allows for greater freedom in designing the whole choreography.

CHAPTER THREE

The Right Music

As mentioned, the music chosen creates the atmosphere. It isn't merely the acoustical background; it forms a true foundation for the entire performance. It must both inspire the rider and thrill the observer-turned-listener. The riders should literally get goosebumps when "their" music begins. For the audience, visual and acoustical perceptions merge into a single experience.

MEASURE AND RHYTHM

In the following discussions of music we will be dealing with two terms which I wish to elucidate: *measure* and *rhythm*. By measure we mean in musical terms the time signature of a particular piece of music, the external framework of an exact, repeating phrase of time. Within a measure we distinguish between the accented and unaccented elements. A measure can be written either in double or triple time whereby the first element, or "beat," is always accented.

Defined musically, rhythm is the temporal relationship of the individual beats within a measure (long to short) as well as the relationship between accented and unaccented beats (light to heavy).

In riding, references to cadence and rhythm retain their musical meanings. Cadence (measure) is an exactly regulated pattern of strides or steps; by rhythm a rider refers to the relationship of the steps to one another within the pattern. Horses have a four-beat walk. If this four-beat rhythm of the gait is interrupted, or if it is not precisely even, as in a lateral walk, this is an error in rhythm even though riders often speak of an error in cadence.

Of cadence in riding we know that the walk is a four-beat, the trot a two-beat, and the canter a three-beat sequence. This would be easy to hear if we were riding on a hard surface such as a road. Our task here is to get the music to fit these cadences. The seeming magic of the circus where the horses dance exactly in time with the music is an illusion. It is the music that matches the cadence of the horses' gaits.

In most cases it just won't be possible to get all the horses moving exactly in time with one another. Thus, we must work with the average tempo, or even better, that of the lead horses as they will be seen first. The results will be approximately as follows:

Walk:	Walk steps per minute	100–115
Trot:	Trot steps per minute	
	Working Trot	156–168
	Collected Trot	148–156
Canter:	Canter strides per minute	
	Working Canter	100
	Collected Canter	90

What we need then is a piece of music that, given some variance, would lie between these values. Disappointingly, it will happen sometimes that music you remember as being ideal will count a hurried 185 trot steps and only 70 canter strides per minute. Small differences can be worked out using the speed regulator found on most record players. You won't want to overuse this tool, however, as notes will begin to waver if drawn out too long.

I have found it aesthetically less disturbing when the tempo of the music is slightly faster than that of the horses than the other way around. A happy Suppé melody or a snappy one by Offenbach, though faster than the tempo of the horses' gait, will be well received and can often increase the impulsion of the horses. It's important not to try to be overly exact in these calculations. Rely on your feel for what is correct. In general, effervescent or suspenseful pieces will lend themselves better to being sped up, whereas classical, dancelike, ceremonial melodies can be drawn out a bit more slowly.

THE WALK

The walk sequence should be done to music that matches this tempo, which means about 100 to 115 beats a minute.

THE TROT

Choice of music for the work at the trot does not necessarily need to be confined to melodies in an accented duple time like Parlow's well-known *Amboss Polka*, which demonstrates a precise, hammering trot rhythm: *one–two, one–two, one–two*. Let's keep in mind, though, that the polka per se is well-suited music for the trot. This is especially the case because polka music often uses the ideal trot tempo of about 160 beats per minute.

We can also find excellent trot music if we explore pieces in triple time. We'll just need to be careful that these aren't accented too heavily on the first note of the measure. The *Wooden Shoe Dance* from the operetta *Zar und Zimmermann (Czar and Carpenter)* by Lortzing is a good example of triple time in which all three beats are accented almost equally. A piece in ¾ time played to a metronome set at fifty-two will give us approximately 156 trot steps per minute. Thus, in selecting trot music in ¾ time, count the number of measures and multiply by three. A waltz with sixty measures will then give us 180 trot steps (depending on the horse).

In the more advanced performances, such as the individual kur, the pas de deux, or the pas de quatre, pronounced, hammering trot rhythms such as the *Amboss Polka* are best not used. Here the waltzing ¾ time with its 150–160 beats per minute seems especially well suited.

THE CANTER

Three-quarter time, waltz time, comes to mind for the canter as long as the tempo fits. Unfortunately, most of the lovely concert waltzes with their 60–80 beats per minute are too slow for our purposes. We will need a tempo of about 90–100 beats per minute. If the waltz tempo lies under 60, it might well be suitable for the trot.

Also, I would like to distinguish between waltzes like the well-known *Snow Waltz*, that are patterned after the waltz's original form, the old German "Spinner," and the concert and symphonic waltzes from opera and ballet. The older form, the rather monotonous "Spinner" with its repetitive *um*-pa-pa, *um*-pa-pa, is not very useful to us here. The second form, however, is quite dynamic and full of gracefully choreographic elements.

A third form in ¾ time is the minuet. This is usually slower than the waltz and, because this dance is more or less processional in nature, the three beats are more evenly accented. Thus, the minuet, even though in ¾ time, is very well suited for the trot. This is true, practically without exception, of the minuet of the classical era.

Nothing, however, underscores a classical quadrille more beautifully than the animating, elegant, easy-to-listen-to concert waltzes like Gounod's *Faust Waltzes* from the opera *Faust,* and Weber's *Invitation to the Dance.* Here, too, it is important that the music chosen fits the 90–100 canter strides per minute required.

Another tempo that works well for the canter is 4/4 time or a ¾ time with the following basic rhythm: ta-ta-tum, ta-ta-tum, ta-ta-tum.

You will find this good cantering rhythm often in works by Auber such as the operettas *Fra Diavolo, La Muette de Portici, The Black Domino,* and others. If it is the dance element that dominates the concert waltz form, then it is the extraordinarily interesting rhythmical elements that hold our interest in this music. It is also the same rhythm found in the old military canter marches.

The next question of interest might be, Where in the canter pattern should the accent of the music fall? I feel we should be quite content if we have found music that matches the three-beat cadence of the canter and that also fits the timing of the canter stride. Especially since not all horses will be exactly matched in their stride, we won't attach too much importance to this question of accent. The rider of the individual kur, however, will want to deal with these finer points, and discussions of this can be widely found in the theoretical literature of dressage.

CHAPTER FOUR

Sketching Out
the Quadrille

Before proceeding further in our consideration of the proper music to choose, we'll want to lay out a rough sketch of our quadrille and point out a few more technical details.

ENTRANCE AND SALUTE

A quadrille can begin either with the riders organizing outside the arena and then entering single file or in pairs, or with the riders mustering in the arena itself. It is much more impressive to have the riders enter in formation, but this does carry with it the risk that the horses will become distracted by the change of scenery, a problem which forming in the arena does eliminate.

The common formations for the group salute are the straight line, the echelon, and the half-circle. For upper-level quadrilles, I would recommend entering single file and saluting from the center line while in motion. The highest levels should enter at the trot or the canter. It goes without saying that the salute should be done facing the judges or the grandstand.

Depending on the kind of salute, we will need two kinds of music. For the entrance and salute at the halt, we'll need a piece of music of about one minute in length. As there are hardly any compositions this short, we'll have to edit the final theme and ending from a suitable piece, whereby it is important that the music chosen ends with a fitting final chord for the salute.

EXAMPLES: Handel: *Water Music* or *Music for the Royal Fireworks*
Verdi: *Triumphal March* from the opera *Aida*
Suppé: Introduction to the *Light Cavalry Overture*

If the salute is to take place while the file is in motion down the center line, we'll need a selection that runs until the transition to the next gait is to take place. An entrance at the walk should not be carried beyond two minutes, nor is it desirable here, as it was in the first instance, to find music which has a clearly recognizable closing chord.

TRANSLATING PLAYING TIME
TO DISTANCE IN METERS

For our first example, we'll create the format for an easy quadrille at Training or First Level. We have decided on the following gait sequence: walk, trot, canter, trot with final line-up and salute.

The simplest solution to selecting the music would be to buy a recording of marches made especially for riding, for example, Ariola-Eurodisc #218 and #271. We would then choose the pieces we wanted to use and measure the playing time with a stopwatch. Most records and tapes list the playing time for each piece. Next we'll have to calculate which figures we can integrate into this given interval. This is done by measuring the time needed to ride the periphery of the arena, the large circle, and the volté in all three gaits. At the lower levels, the volté should be ridden to the center line. Also we'll be rounding out all calculations to whole meters. For example, the 20-meter circle in a 20 × 40-meter arena is never ridden all the way to the wall. Thus we'll not calculate 20 × 3.14 (π), but we'll round it out to 20 × 3 = 60 meters.

For the regulation 20 × 40-meter arena, we will get the following approximate measurements:*

	Whole Arena	20-Meter Circle	10-Meter Circle
Walk	60 sec.	30 sec.	15 sec.
Trot	35 sec.	20 sec.	10 sec.
Canter	25 sec.	15 sec.	5 sec.

Translator's Note: These measurements reflect meters ridden rather than absolute mathematical calculations. Times cited are averages as an absolute does not exist. I have rounded numbers to the nearest multiple of five.

This means that at the walk to cover the whole arena, or a distance of 120 meters, we'll need 60 seconds; the 20-meter circle, or a distance of 60 meters, we'll need 30 seconds; and the 10-meter circle, or a distance of 30 meters, we'll need 15 seconds.

Let's assume that the entrance music is 2 minutes, 10 seconds long. This is a total of 130 seconds and means that 260 meters of figures at the walk can be ridden. We will proceed similarly to measure for the trot and canter figures.

In the transition from one gait to another, it is best to choose a fairly simple figure, like the whole arena or the 20-meter circle, which will help to even out timing differences. The horses then pick up the trot as soon as the first measure of trot music starts.

A similar procedure is used at the close. An alternative figure is practiced in the sequence just before the final salute and held ready for use. Which of the two possible closing figures is actually used in the performance is decided in the last moment and calculated so that the salute comes exactly with the final chord of the music.

This is the basic framework used to prepare for all musical presentations: select the level of difficulty, determine the sequence of the gaits, find suitable music, then work the individual figures into the playing time of the music selected.

CHAPTER FIVE

Types of Music

Musicality is inborn; the greater the musicality and sensitivity of the quadrille director, the more certain the selection of just the right music, and thus the more successful the final product. If you doubt your abilities in this area, it would be wise to ask the counsel of someone more knowledgeable in the field. A broad knowledge of what is available is also necessary, and a definite boon, of course, would be a large personal library of records or tapes.

If you wish to combine several different pieces of music for the quadrille, these should complement each other in kind and in terms of the instrumentalization and atmosphere each creates. The following contrasts are too stark:

- Monumental symphonic music and delicate piano etudes
- Classical music and jazz
- Works by Bach and Stravinsky

In the previous chapter we used only traditional riding marches for our first sample quadrille. Of course it is possible to combine works by several composers, again, as long as the pieces complement one another.

MARCHES AND POLKAS

The golden age of Viennese Operetta has provided us with a cornucopia of rhythmical and tuneful melodies suited for the quadrille. Pieces by Strauss, Lanner, Ziehrer, Suppé, Millöcker, and Hellmesberger can be combined nicely.

Johann Strauss, Sr. left an oeuvre of more than 250 works. His son, Johann Strauss, Jr., doubled this output. His *Emperor's Waltz* is an almost symphonic creation. Richard Wagner called Strauss, Jr., "the most musical mind of the nineteenth centry." Josef and Eduard Strauss round out the Viennese period. A large selection of marches, polkas, and waltzes from this era are particulary suitable for the quadrille.

What could be imaginably nicer than an all-Strauss quadrille?

Strauss Quadrille		min/sec
Entrance at the Walk	Entrance march from *The Gypsy Baron*	2.40
Trot	*Annen Polka*	4.00
	Tritsch-Tratsch Polka	2.40
Canter and Final Salute	*The Blue Danube Waltz*	3.15
		12.35
Exit at the Walk	*Radetzky March*	

Many would see this as the ideal quadrille. It almost seems that Strauss himself calculated this polka-trot rhythm with its 160 beats per minute with the quadrille in mind. For this we are very thankful to the venerable Waltz King.

As to marches, we need to point out the difference between the Austrian and Prussian marches. The Austrian marches, even those written expressly for the military, are not quite as brisk, nor quite as rigid, as are the Prussian marches. They seem, instead, more dancelike and exude a definite nonchalance, especially when played by an Austrian band such as the Tyrolean Regimental Band or the Zell Town Musicians.

BALLET MUSIC

Here, too, we can differentiate between two types. On the one hand is the actual ballet as musical theater where the entire drama is danced without a chorus or vocal soloists. The well-known Russian composer Tchaikovsky provides a good example of such ballet drama with his works *Swan Lake, The Nutcracker,* and *The Sleeping Beauty.*

The second type is the incidental ballet music from grand opera for which the French are largely to thank. In contrast to Italian opera composers of the Romantic era such as Rossini and Bellini, who rarely included incidental ballet music, the French had firmly ensconced the ballet as an integral part of grand opera from the time of the baroque. Those who aspired to write for the French opera stage of the time had to follow the house rules in this regard. The French public expected a ballet in every opera. This usually came in the third act to accommodate that goodly number of people who typically came late to the performance. The ballet was the high point of the evening. Thus it was that other composers would include extensive ballet pieces in operas intended for Paris, or added ballet to existing operas when these were to be performed on the French stage. It is this French ballet tradition that we have to thank for the very lovely ballet music found in the operas of Donizetti, Tchaikovsky, and Verdi.

For many who haven't listened to much of it, the very term "classical music" might carry overtones of cultural snobbishness. It conjures up images of children from better families who take piano lessons or sissies with violin cases under their arms. My ventures into the realms of opera and ballet in search of quadrille music were also often ridiculed. For those of you who have not had much exposure to classical music, I would ask you to set aside any prejudices and listen. Ballet music is classified as a form of classical, symphonic music and even those who have no background in this music at all will enjoy it. Just as the top hat and tails belong to upper level dressage, so classical music belongs to the upper level quadrille.

SYMPHONIC MUSIC

In introduction, a symphony is an orchestral work written in three or four "movements," usually in the following pattern: a slow first movement, followed by a dancelike second movement—often in the form of a minuet —and concluding with a fast final movement. Among symphonies, the works of Beethoven, Haydn, and Mozart stand out. It is with these that we will mostly concern ourselves.

When Haydn died in 1809 at the age of seventy-seven, he left behind 104 symphonies in addition to a large oeuvre of chamber music. Mozart wrote 46 symphonies. Even from just these two composers, then, we have quite a selection to choose from.

For a Training Level quadrille, I wouldn't choose symphonic music. But from First Level on, plan to use it. I always find the ¾-time minuets interesting, and these often fit the tempo requirements for the trot. Listen to the following symphonies to see if they fit your choreographic ideas:

Beethoven   Symphony no. 3 in E-flat Major (*Eroica*), 1st and 3rd Movements

Symphony no. 5 in C Minor, 1st and 3rd Movements

Symphony no. 8 in F Major, 1st and 2nd Movements

Egmont Overture

Handel	*Water Music*
	Music for the Royal Fireworks

Haydn	Symphony no. 93 in D Major
	Symphony no. 94 in G Major (*The Surprise*)
	Symphony no. 101 in D Major (*The Clock*), Minuet: Trot (150).

Mozart	Symphony in E-flat Major, K. 543, Minuet: Trot.
	Symphony no. 35 in D Major, (*Haffner*), K. 385. 1st Movement (Allegro): Trot (160).
	Symphony no. 41 in G Minor, (*Jupiter*), K. 551. 1st Movement: Trot (152); 2nd Movement: Trot (162); 4th Movement: Canter (120).
	March in D Major, K. 408.2: Walk.
	Horn Concerto in D Major, K. 412: Walk.

These few examples are intended, for now, to serve just as an introductory sampling to show that symphonic music is very usable for the quadrille, especially where the riders' abilities are correspondingly developed.

Before proceeding, I have a few more basic remarks:

1. The tempos that I have given for the above-mentioned works, for example, trot (160) and canter (100), were taken from the records I worked with. Because different conductors will vary in their directing, you will, of course, need to check this and measure the tempos for yourself.

2. If you find it necessary to combine several pieces, you cannot just stop a selection in some arbitrary place. Ideally you will allow the musical phrase to come to an end. Should time considerations not permit this, or if parts of the section are not very suitable, try to maintain the musical integrity of the piece by shortening it at repetitions, at breaks, or at the end of a phrase. Never tear apart a musical thought, unit, or theme.

POPULAR MUSIC

Now that we've discussed the various genres of major interest here—riding marches, polkas, waltzes, ballet, and symphonies—we'll turn also to more modern arrangements and popular music. Orchestrated versions of popular tunes and dance music can, of course, also be used. The fox trot with its 2/4 or 4/4 rhythm is very suitable. Such catchy, popular tunes would also be ideal for a New Year's or Fasching's ride. Popular arrangements of classics are also very useful. Excellent examples are Richard Clayderman's dreamy, playful melodies. Oldtime jazz and ragtime rhythms can also be very useful. Again, however, I must repeat that whatever combinations are made, the pieces must complement each other, for the music sets the mood for the entire performance.

THE TEST RIDE

After considerable searching and finally finding "your" music, you conclude this phase in the planning process. Next, record the pieces in order onto a practice tape and ride to it. You'll probably find some selections to be disappointments, while others will work out quite excitingly. Keep in mind that the music will sound very different in the school than it did in your living room, and you'll note a further change in the sound effects in moving from the indoor school to the outdoor arena. Thus it could happen that after your test ride, you'll have to resume your search for music that truly embodies your ideas, until, in some moment of great good luck, you find exactly what you need and can say, "That's it! That will be our music."

THE QUADRILLE
WITH CONTINUOUS MUSIC

Until now we've been considering fusing shorter pieces which complement each other and which are appropriate to the various gaits. There is, of course, an alternative. We can look for single works in which the rhythms for all three gaits occur and that we could, then, play through in the original. We'll need to watch that the playing time runs between ten and fifteen minutes, that the gaits won't have to be changed too often, and that there won't be too much done at the walk. It might also be necessary in such pieces to carefully excise a somewhat boring section. There aren't too many pieces that fit this description, but what does exist can be lovely and is quite interesting music to work with. Indeed, I find these original compositions to be the best form of quadrille music as the music and the ridden figures can be made to blend most harmoniously. To this genre belong, in first place, overtures from operas and operettas, unified thematic wholes that often contain very suitable entrance music and conclusions that can absolutely compel an audience to its feet.

Opera Overtures

The nineteenth century is also known as the Era of the Grand Opera. At the hub was the city of Paris, which was also home to many important composers in the first half of that century: Auber, Adam, Bellini, Berlioz, Boieldieu, Cherubini, Chopin, Donizetti, Gounod, Liszt, Meyerbeer, Rossini, Verdi, and Wagner. It is hard to imagine the overwhelming musical genius that concentrated itself in Paris at this time. All these names also catalog a list of overtures which are suitable for our use. Adolphe Adam alone composed fifty-three operas, including *Le Postillon de Longjumeau, The Nurnberg Doll*, and *La Reine d'un jour*. In choosing suitable quadrille music, make sure to take a closer look at the following composers:

Auber	*The Black Domino*
	La Muette de Portici
	The Bronze Horse
	Fra Diavolo
	The Crown Diamonds
Adam	*The Nurnberg Doll*
Mozart	*Cosi fan tutte*
	The Abduction from the Seraglio
	The Marriage of Figaro
Rossini	*The Italian Woman in Algiers*
	The Barber of Seville
	The Silken Ladder
	The Thieving Magpie
	Semiramide

The Parisian Operetta

Towards the middle of the nineteenth century began the triumphal march of the Parisian operetta. The operetta overture, like its operatic counterpart, is very suitable for the quadrille. The main difference between the two is that the operetta overture often has a more sprightly, indeed almost irreverent, frivolous tune that is wonderfully suitable for quadrilles at the lower levels.

The great master of this time was Jacques Offenbach. He wrote music that bubbles over with sensuous delights. He is known as the "inventor" of the cancan rhythm with its concomitant spicy and impudent Moulin Rouge atmosphere dramatized by ruffled skirts and black net stockings held by bright red garters. The following Offenbach overtures belong on our list: *Orpheus in the Underworld, The Grand Duchess of Gerolstein, The Beautiful Helena, Bluebeard,* and *Parisian Life.*

The Viennese Operetta

The Viennese operetta had its origin in the prosaic Biedermeier farce from the Vienna of the 1830s. Its beginning was more romantic and touching in character than its Parisian counterpart. In its further development, the Viennese operetta became the embodiment of that Viennese melting pot of hot-blooded Hungarian, Baltic, and Slavic folk music. At the time when in Paris the name Offenbach was beginning its rise to fame, in Vienna the name of Franz von Suppé began to glimmer, a name that in the last part of the century was to light up the heavens of the Viennese operetta. With his elegant and masterfully worked operettas he drew the first outlines for what was to become the classical Viennese operetta. This golden age was then to be hallmarked by yet another famous name—Johann Strauss. From Suppé we find the following overtures of interest: *The Beautiful Galathea, Poet and Peasant, Light Cavalry, A Day in Vienna, Queen of Spades, The Gigilo, Fatinitza,* and *Boccaccio.*

Take the time also to explore the riches of the other Viennese operettas. Johann Strauss is paramount here with *Die Fledermaus, The Gypsy Baron, Viennese Blood,* and *A Night in Vienna.* Other masters of the era are:

Zeller	*Der Vogelhandler*
Millocker	*Poor John*
	Der Bettelstudent
	Gasparone
Hellmesberger	*The Oracle* (very famous ball scenes)
Ziehrer	*The Vagrant.*
Heuberger	*An Opera Ball*

Lanner (who wrote many lovely waltzes)

Indeed this category of Viennese operetta contains much unexplored territory well worth your attention.

The Berlin Operetta

I can't bring this discussion to a close without mentioning the blossoming of the Berlin operetta from its cabaret origins at the turn of the century. It never quite attained the fame and glory of the Parisian or Viennese operetta; nevertheless, thanks to its warm folkish quality, it remained very popular through the 1950s. At the head of the troup of Berlin operetta composers is that master Paul Linke, who from 1847 to 1899 had directed the orchestra of the Folies Bèrgeres and had brought with him to Berlin some of that Offenbach sparkle. *Frau Luna, Lysistrata,* and *Grigri* are his best-known works.

It was Walter Kollo, though, who best captured the special tone of Berlin. He wrote nearly forty operettas. His best-known works include *The Joke Baron, As Once in May,* and *Three Old Wrecks.* We can round out this portrait of the Berlin composers with the names Gilbert, Jessel, and Künneke.

I would imagine that riders from the Berlin area would be especially drawn to this music, given its strong foothold in local folk melodies which seem ideal. Among these are:

Glow Worm: Trot

Berliner Air: Walking March

Sports Palace Waltz: Slow Trot

It was in Schöneberg: Trot or Canter

CHAPTER SIX

From Theory
to Practice

One well-known rider's motto is, "You learn how to ride only by riding; however, knowledge of the underlying theory predicates all success."

In these past chapters, I've tried to impart to my readers some theoretical basis for the selection of music for the quadrille. Let's expand upon this a bit before proceeding with an overview of suitable quadrille music. Specifically, let's work through the musical plan for an entire quadrille performance. In doing this, I will be demonstrating the procedures I have been able to use successfully in my own work. For this example, we're looking for a sprightly, gay piece suitable for a First Level quadrille. I've chosen such a piece from a recording of Offenbach overtures: *The Beautiful Helena*. Assemble all the tools we need—paper, pencil, and stopwatch—and we can begin. First, let's set up the following diagram and then start the record.

Offenbach: *The Beautiful Helena*

Total mins.	Atmosphere created	Fitting gait	Playing time
0	Good entrance	Walk	0.35
0.35	Rather calm (too?)	Walk	0.45
1.20	Good dynamic crescendo	Trot (180)	1.35
2.55	Tutti, bounding	Canter (90)	0.50
3.45	Pause	?	0.15

4.00	Dancelike trot (oboes)	Trot	0.50
4.50	Forte!!	Trot	0.30
5.20	Piano	Walk or turns	0.40
6.00	Melody—dynamic theme	Trot	0.40
6.40	Rhythm! Increasing crescendo	Trot!!	1.05
7.45	Crescendo again		0.20
8.05	Furioso—climax	Canter (100)	0.40
8.45	Finale with Salute		

Without doubt, this is glorious music. How tempting to work with and how interesting a piece, increasing dynamically till the very last chord and with just the right amount of walk time. We'll have to think a bit, however, how we can work around those quieter, slower parts. Perhaps we could build in some turns on the forehand at the walk, or a leg yield away from and back to the long side. A figure ridden on the 20-meter circle from B to E would be another solution.

The playing time of 8 minutes, 45 seconds is about the minimum length we can use. It might be good to preface it with another piece during the entrance. Let's return to our Offenbach recording to search for a possible addition. We create the same working format on paper as we used before. In listening to the overtures, we find that all of them have wonderful endings and that the beginnings are fine for the entrance march or for the first figures at the walk, but all of them have rather slow, quiet places in the body of the pieces.

In *Orpheus in the Underworld* the last 3 minutes, 35 seconds are very useful. In *Bluebeard* we find too much rapid change of tempo. From it, we'd only be able to use the first minute for the figures at the walk. In *Parisian Life* we find good walk music about 2 minutes, 20 seconds into the piece, and at 3 minutes, 30 seconds there is good trot music with a tempo of 168 beats that has a dramatic crescendo building to the closing chord at 4 minutes, 45 seconds. This would yield 2 minutes, 25 seconds that would be quite usable. I've now come to the following conclusion:

Entrance and Salute using *Bluebeard*	1.00

Walk and trot using:	
Parisian Life from 2.20 till 4.45	2.25
The Beautiful Helena from 1.20 till the end at 8.45	
(leave off the too-quiet first 1.20)	7.25

Total Time:	10.50

Let's record these three pieces on a trial tape leaving about a 2 seconds break between them, then listen to the whole recording. If we're satisfied with the product, we now have the musical basis for our Offenbach quadrille and can draw up the final plan with actual playing times.

Entrance and Salute, *Bluebeard*   1.00

Total mins.		Atmosphere created	Fitting gait	Playing time

Parisian Life

2.20	= 0	Walk	Walk	1.10
3.30	= 1.10	Trot (168)	Trot (168)	1.15
4.45	= 2.25	End *Parisian Life*		

The Beautiful Helena

1.20	= 2.25	Trot (180)	Trot (180)	1.35
2.55	= 4.00	Tutti and crescendo	Canter (90)	0.50
3.45	= 4.50	Quiet phase		0.15
4.00	= 5.05	Dancelike trot (oboes)	Trot	0.50
4.50	= 5.55	Forte!	Trot	0.30
5.20	= 6.25	Piano	Walk or turns	0.40
6.00	= 7.05	Melody—dynamic theme	Trot	0.40
6.40	= 7.45	Rhythm! Increasing crescendo	Trot!	1.05
7.45	= 8.50	Crescendo again		0.20
8.05	= 9.10	Furioso—climax		0.40
8.45	= 9.50	Final chord and salute		

		Total Playing Time:		9.50

MEDITATION

I can't think of a better description for the next phase of our work than meditation. The task now is to weave our figures into this established musical arrangement, to choreograph the whole. This requires an inner quietude and relaxation conducive to the inspirational muse.

Play the music, relax, close your eyes, and listen. Visualize the riders in the indoor arena. Take your time—lots of time—and play the recording over and over again. Scenes and ridden figures will begin to form in your mind's eye: extentions across the diagonal ridden to a dynamic crescendo, balletlike collection, then swinging fully into the canter, another crescendo leading to the furioso, then the closing formation, halt, and salute!

A lot of time has gone by; you're still sitting, meditating. The contours of the total picture have taken form.

FROM PLAYING TIME
TO METERED DISTANCE

Let's go back for a minute to this problem of translating time to riding distance. Let's use a slightly modified diagram and list the progression of the various figures for our quadrille.

Salute formation facing C (seen from C from left to right: riders 7, 5, 3, 1, 2, 4, 6, and 8)

Lead riders at:	Command	Approximate Ridden Meters	Seconds
X	File, Walk! (8 abreast)	0	
C	Split, 4 right, 4 left	20	
M & H	Change rein through the diagonal in fours	40	
K & F	Single file	85	
A	Down center line in pairs (when the file is on the center line, 140 meters have been ridden in 70 seconds. At this point the trot music begins.)	105	
G	File, Trot!	140	70 seconds walking
G	10-meter circle right & left	30	
C	Split to right & left		
B & E	10-meter circle, then whole arena	A = 130	
F & K	Change rein through the diagonal		
C	Down center line in pairs	X = 230	70 seconds trotting

Up to this point (X), 70 seconds at the walk and 70 seconds at the trot have been ridden. This totals 140 seconds, or 2 minutes, 20 seconds. We can see from our music diagram that the trot from *The Beautiful Helena* begins at this point. Thus we will need an additional 1.40 minutes of work at the trot until the canter work begins at 4.00 minutes.

This method, I hope, will serve to facilitate your working with material and the incorporation of your figures into the music.

Just as we have put together our Offenbach quadrille, works from other composers can be similarly combined.

Mozart

Walk	March in D Major, K. 408.2	2.35
Trot	Minuet from the *Jupiter* Symphony, K. 551	4.20
Canter	Rondo from Horn Concerto in D Major, K. 412	3.20

Approximate breaks between selections 0.05
Total Playing Time: 10.20

Suppé: *Light Cavalry* **Overture**

Use from the beginning with the well-known opening fanfare until 3 minutes, 50 seconds. Cut off at this point and append the whole overture to *The Jolly Robbers*. The fiery finale to this overture is a true treat for the ear.

Auber's overtures can also be easily combined in this manner. Also try combining ballet pieces. There is quite a large selection here for us to use. As mentioned above, however, the individual selections within the overtures are of short duration; therefore, the tempos change rapidly. You'll have to listen carefully to find the useful parts.

Most importantly though, the music must say something to you, awaken your imagination. Let the music fascinate you; let it stimulate your creativity.

CONCLUSION

Even at the risk of being repetitious, I would like to emphasize a few points.

The harmonious accord of the ridden program with the music must be our first priority. By this I don't mean merely the rhythmical synchronization between the horses' gait and the beat of the music. Keep in mind that music orchestrated for smaller groups of instruments and the more delicate, dancelike, serenadelike compositions are more suitable for the pas de deux, pas de quatre, or a ladies' quadrille. The more horses you have in the arena, the more powerful the music must be. Where strings and chamber music seem more suitable in the first instances, here it is the brass—horns, trumpets, trombones—and the percussion instruments—drums and kettle drums—that should dominate.

The volume, too, must fit the choreography. An increase in volume should mean an extention of gait; the quieter the music, the more collected the work should be.

Dance music—the minuet, gavotte, mazurka, and others—invoke curved lines, serpentines, and figures where pairs merge, then divide. Your riders must know this music so perfectly by heart that no spoken commands are necessary. In changing from one gait to another, from trot to canter, for example, the horses should "bound" into the music at the first canter note. The sum of all these factors is a harmonious blending with the music that sustains the figure play of the quadrille.

Over the years, I have collected the musical works listed in the survey appended here, having checked them out in terms of their suitability for the quadrille. The list is intended for your use. By no means is it complete. It is a foundation upon which you can build. Listen to the radio, being constantly alert for possible quadrille music. Look through the weekly listings for appropriate programs and listen to channels that usually play suitable music. These listings are often given by genre, i.e., overtures, ballet music, brass music of the baroque. Invididual selections are often specifically named. If you're traveling, you can do this with your car radio. Keep a writing pad handy to note any interesting recordings.

For birthdays and other gift-giving occasions you'll soon find yourself with a "wish list" of recordings. I would also suggest that you draw up a chart for the music you collect. This could be organized as follows:

Composer/Title/Atmosphere/Gait/Time Signature/Playing Time

Perhaps you could add another column for your remarks, giving each piece a score for appropriateness ranging from "excellent" to "unsuitable."

In time you will develop a sense for rhythm and timing so that even without a stopwatch or counting beats per minute, you'll be able to tell a 148 from a 160 trot rhythm. It helps if you are a supple rider with a swinging back and a sense of rhythm who rides every day. (I am actually presuming this to be the case and am embarrassed even to mention it.)

I'd also like to say a few words about the rehearsals. Ideally your quadrille riders would also be your dressage students and the horses would carry the stamp of your training. I know, however, that this is hardly ever the case, and that you'll be working with whatever is available.

Quadrille work usually begins in the fall after the show season has ended. In the summer many riders are away at shows and have to school their horses for these, or they do a lot of trail riding, enjoying the sun, open sky, and nature in general with their horses. Vacation time, when many people are on trips, is also lost to us. Thus it is not until October or November that our quadrille practice can begin in earnest. I've found weekend mornings seem a good time to get everyone together. You'll find, too, that the practice sessions will draw quite a crowd of interested onlookers.

Before actual practice begins, the riders should meet unmounted to discuss the work ahead. The individual figures and their sequence can be drawn on a blackboard. Later each figure, for example the entrance and salute, and the walk figures, is practiced individually without music. As a treat then, these figures could be ridden to music to end the first session.

If the quadrille is to be performed for a special occasion, a show, or a holiday program, then work must begin in earnest and rehearsals held at least once a week. It is now that mental images must take on the firm contours of reality. The riders' abilities must be polished and the impulsion of the horses must be improved.

Familiarize your riders with the music. They shouldn't just ride, but must also learn to listen and to translate what they hear into motion. You'll have to help here. As a conductor directs his orchestra, you must inspire your riders to "play" their instrument—the horse. You have designed the choreography; now you must bring these ideas into being through your artists—horse and rider.

Always keep the image in back of your mind that we want to dance with our horses. Dance, harmony, beauty—this is what you must awaken in your riders.

> "Perfect harmony between rider and horse—in other words, beauty—is the final goal of all dressage. One must be able to recognize in the horse a feeling of well-being and yet, at the same time, not detect in the rider any indication of how difficult that path has been."
>
> Wilhelm Müseler

CHAPTER SEVEN

A Survey of Music for the Quadrille

AN OVERVIEW OF GENRES

Marches: Military March, Riding March, Entrance March, Ceremonial Formations, Solemn Processions

Polkas

Waltzes: Viennese Waltz, Concert Waltz

Opera Overtures

Operetta Overtures

Symphonic Music

Ballet Music

Music for the Pas de Deux and Pas de Quatre

Miscellaneous

NOTE: The tempos per minute given here are accurate for the recordings I had at my disposal. These may change from conductor to conductor. I have found differences in the trot rhythm ranging from 152 to 172 in different recordings of the same piece. Thus, before making a purchase, listen to the various recordings of a selection in the listening booth. In this way you can select the version that comes closest to the tempo you need.

Music suitable for smaller groups and the individual kur are noted with an asterisk (*).

Translator's Note: Throughout this section, tempos are given in parenthesis; playing times in minutes and seconds are indicated as whole numbers and decimals. For example, 2.34 = 2 minutes, 34 seconds.

THE MOST IMPORTANT MUSICAL TERMS

Adagio	slow, easy
Allegretto	lively
Allegro	brisk, lively, happy
Andante	"walking," moderately slow
Cancan	a wild, fast dance originating in Algeria
Capriccio	a fanciful, lively composition
Chord	several notes played simultaneously
Choreography	symbolic representation or arrangement of dance figures
Con brio	"with brilliance," lively
Finale	closing movement
Forte	loud, intense
Harmony	pleasing agreement of tones played simultaneously
Intrade	introductory music to older operas, today known as the overture
Krakowiak	Polish national dance in 2/4 time
Laendler	slow, waltzlike dance in 3/4 time
Largo	very slow, broad
Major	gay, happy tone characteristic of major keys
Mazurka	Polish national dance in 3/4 time
Minor	soft, sad tone characteristic of minor keys
Minuet	courtly dance of French origin in moderate 3/4 time
Moderato	moderate
Nocturne	night music
Overture	musical preface to operas, operettas, and plays
Piano	soft, tender
Polka	Bohemian national dance in 3/4 time
Polonaise	Polish national dance in 3/4 time
Presto	hurried, fast
Quadrille	French square dance in five rounds to different time signatures
Rhapsody	improvised composition
Rondo	composition with recurring refrain
Scherzo	lively, sprightly, humorous
Serenade	night music
Tarantella	extremely lively Italian dance in 3/8 or 6/8 time
Tutti	all, the whole orchestra
Vivace	lively

MARCHES

Forty years have passed since the last, terrible World War. This should be time enough to allow us to reinstate the discredited march in riding circles. There is so much dancelike, happy music in the march. It sets the listener afire and heralds the start of something important. You don't have to use that favorite of the Third Reich, *The Badenweiler March*, or *The Glory of Prussia*.

Entrance and Exit Marches

Strauss, Sr.	*Radetzky March*
Strauss, Jr.	*Persian March*
Suppe	*Oh, my Austria*
Schrammel	*Vienna Forever*
Spohr	*Salute to Kiel*
Leonhard	*Prince Eugen*
Beethoven	*York March*
	Kaertner Melodies
Kopetzky	*Egerland March*
Krettner	*Toelzian Sharpshooters March*
Neudel	*Prince Karl March*
	March of the Swiss Guard
Alford	*Colonel Bogey March*

Canter Marches

Strauss, Sr.	*Radetzky March*
Suppé	*Light Cavalry*

Solemn Processionals

Beethoven	March from Symphony no. 3, 2nd Movement

Ceremonial Exit and Entrance Marches

Beethoven — Tatoo in C Major no. 2. Good entrance march at the trot (148).

Handel — *Music for the Royal Fireworks*. Grave (Overture): ceremonious introduction. La Rejouissance: 4/4 time; great entrance. La Paix: stately hymn, similar to the tatoo. Minuet 2: ceremonial exit.

Haydn, Michael — *Turkish March* in C Major. Swinging march, suitable for entrance at the walk (120).

Liszt	*Les Préludes.* Ending suitable for grand final formation and salute.
Meyerbeer	*Torch Dance no. 1.* Stately entrance at the trot (168) or at the canter (84). Playing time: 5.25.
Monteverdi	Overture to *Orfeo.* Ceremonial fanfare and entrance march.
Mozart	March in D Major, K. 408.2.* For the walk. Playing time: 3.37.
Purcell	*Trumpet Voluntary.* Imposing entrance march. [Note: this piece is actually by Jeremiah Clark.]
Strauss, Johann, Jr.	Entrance march from *The Gypsy Baron* (2.44) *Persian March* (2.20) *Egyptian March* (3.50)
Strauss, Richard	*Also sprach Zarathustra.* First measures begin with a powerful theme played by the brass.
Tchaikovsky	*Capriccio italien.* First measures are very suitable for a quick final formation.
	Wedding March. A polonaise from *Eugene Onegin.* Good canter entrance (96). Playing time: 4.40.
	Marche Slav, opus 31. From 2.15 till the end at 8.40 is good walk, trot finale.
Verdi	*Triumphal March* from *Aida.* Grand and stately entrance march.

Trot Marches

Recordings of these are often available in riding specialty stores.

>*Gentlemen's Night Out Polka*
>*Garde du Corps*
>*Dragoon Regiment no. 2*
>*Giselle*
>*Hanoverian Garde du Corps*
>*I heard the rippling of a stream*
>*Der Jäger aus Kurpfalz*

These trot marches are also very suitable for driving demonstrations, especially with coaches of four.

POLKAS

These folk dances in 2/4 time provide limitless accompaniment for our work at the trot.

Strauss, Johann, Sr. *Annen Polka*

Strauss, Johann, Jr. *Tritsch-Tratsch Polka*
Peasants' Polka
Thunder and Lightning Polka
Leichtes Blut
Perpetual Motion

Strauss, Joseph   *Fire Festival*

Parlow   *Amboss Polka*

VIENNESE AND CONCERT WALTZES

We've already spoken a lot about the use of the waltz. So many melodies, catchy Viennese waltzes, are available played at various tempos, which makes them suitable both for the trot and the canter. The instrumentalization and dynamism of the pieces inspire an interesting choreography. Don't limit yourself always to *The Blue Danube Waltz*. Johann Strauss wrote so many absolute gems of waltzes.

Strauss, Johann, Jr. *Morning Newspapers*
Roses from the South
Tales from the Vienna Woods
Wine, Women and Song
Emperor's Waltz
Waldmeister
Freut Euch des Lebens

Strauss, Josef   *Austrian Village Swallows*

Lanner   *The Citizens of Schoenbrunn*
Court Ball Dances

Ziehrer   *Viennese Citizens*

SYMPHONIC WALTZES

Gounod   *Faust Waltzes* from *Faust*. Canter (72). Playing
time: 4.19.

Tchaikovsky	Waltzes from *The Sleeping Beauty*. Canter (70). Playing time: 4.35.
	Waltzes from *Swan Lake*. Suitable for trot and canter. Playing time: 6.60.
	Waltzes from *Eugene Onegin*. Canter (72). Playing time: 6.30.
Weber	*Invitation to the Dance*. Canter (85).

OPERATIC OVERTURES

Auber	*La Muette de Portici*. Very nice trot music (160–68); canter finale (92). Playing time: 8.15.
	*The Black Domino.** Interesting music with a dazzling canter (75–100) for a pas de deux or other smaller groups.
	The Bronze Horse. Good trot music (140 and 160); wonderful canter (100). Playing time: 7.40.
	*Fra Diavolo.** Very interesting, grand canter music lasting 5.10. Total playing time: 8.30.
	The Crown Diamonds. Superb entrance at the walk from 3.15. Playing time: 8.50.
Boieldieu	*The Calif of Bagdad*. Walk 2.00; good trot (152–60). Trot time: 5.30. Total playing time, walk and trot: 7.30.
Ferrari, Wolf	*Susanna's Secret*. Continuous, snappy trot music (152).
Glinka	*Ruslan and Ludmilla*. Continuous trot rhythm (160); sprightly beginning; quiet middle section. Playing time: 4.55.
Herold	*Zampa*
Mozart	Overtures; see under "Symphonic Music"
Rossini	*The Thieving Magpie*. Grand entrance at the walk (112); wonderful trot melody with a dynamic crescendo to the canter (172). Playing time: 9.40.
	The Italian Woman in Algiers. Quiet introduction at the walk; trot work (152–60 increasing to 172). Playing time: 7.15.

The Barber of Seville. Quiet walk introduction (96), trot (172), and very good canter (112). Playing time: 7.30.

The Silken Ladder. Quiet introduction, then main tempo at 120; not too useful. Playing time: 6.05.

Semiramide. Begins quietly and thinly. Then follow 3.50 of trot (158) with a lovely crescendo to a grandiose close. Playing time: 11.35.

William Tell. After the minute-long cello introduction comes a suitable 1.30 canter (96), followed by a racy trot (160), concluding then with 3.05 of canter.

The Journey to Reims. Superb canter music (95–100) in the second half of the overture.

Rimsky-Korsakov   *Russian Easter Overture.* Very lovely trot music (152). Overwhelming finale!

Smetana   *The Two Widows.* Good trot music with canter finale.

(See also "Symphonic Music" for other overtures.)

OPERETTA OVERTURES

Offenbach   *Orpheus in the Underworld.* Short trot introduction to a lovely melody; the closing two minutes are wonderful for the trot (168); everything in between is unsuitable.

The Grand Duchess of Gerolstein. Very interesting. Good walk march at approximately 0.55. From the 4 minute mark till the end at 6.35, grand trot (144–52) with a racy finish. 2.35 of trot.

The Beautiful Helena. Very useful for walk, trot, and canter. Furious finish. Playing time: 8.45.

Bluebeard. Very nice walk entrance; quiet trot. Interesting music but the tempo changes frequently.

Parisian Life. I highly recommend this short overture. Trot (160), canter (95). Playing time: 4.35.

Heuberger   *An Opera Ball.* Gay, sprightly trot music.

Suppé   Light Cavalry. Powerful fanfare for entrance at the walk. Excepting the slower middle section, the entire overture is a single, almost folkish trot melody with a sweeping rhythm. Unfortunately, its 140 tempo is a little slow. Playing time: 7.34.

Queen of Spades. Quiet introduction for the walk (86); good trot (160) from 3.05; quiet section from 5.15 till 6.50. From this point is a wonderful close at the trot (160) and the canter (100). Playing time: 8.15.

A Day in Vienna. Except for the lovely ending, rather uninteresting.

The Jolly Robbers. Fanfare for entrance at walk or canter (96). From 1.20 there's a lovely section for work at the walk, followed by suitable sections varying for trot and canter. Playing time: 7.05.

*Poet and Peasant.** Except for the cello introduction, suitable for the pas de deux.

Strauss, Johann, Jr. *Die Fledermaus*.* Could probably be used for the pas de deux. The last 2 minutes are very good for trot and canter.

SYMPHONIC MUSIC

Abel

Symphony in E-flat Major.* Similar to chamber music. Suitable for the pas de deux. First movement: trot (144); third movement: canter (80).

Auber

Tarantella from *La Muette de Portici*. Very sprightly trot music.

Bach, Johann
   Christian

Symphony in B-flat Major, opus 9 no. 1. Trot (152) music in the final movement.

Beethoven

Symphony no. 3, *Eroica*. First movement: trot (148); second movement: solemn procession; third movement: canter (108); fourth movement: suitable for walk and trot with the final 50 seconds moving to a heroic close.

Symphony no. 5, the *Fate* symphony. First movement: trot (174); the third movement brings a monumentally heroic trot (164).

Symphony no. 8. First movement: very good trot (162); the second movement also offers a marvelous trot (160); last movement trot (140).

Egmont Overture. Suitable throughout for trot work (164).

Overture in C Major, *The Consecration of the House*. First part is suitable as a hymn or solemn march. Second part is a ceremonial entrance march at the walk; third section: trot music (144). Fourth section is a fugue (128), not too useful.

Eleven Viennese Dances. Just beautiful music! Wonderful for the pas de deux. Everything is in 3/4 time, but nevertheless good for walk, trot, and canter.

Berlioz   *Hungarian March* from *La Damnation de Faust*. There are about 6 minutes of powerful trot music (160).

Bizet   *L'Arlésienne*, Suite no. 1. Quite a bit here is usable.

Carmen, prelude to Act 1. Very well known melody. Good walk music.

Cherubini   Overture to *Anacréon*. From about the second minute through till the end: good trot (152). Playing time: 10:00.

Enescu   *Rumanian Rhapsody no. 1*. Hungarian gypsy music written for full orchestra; the last 6 minutes are very good for trot (160).

Handel   *Music for the Royal Fireworks*. Grave: ceremonial entrance at the walk; could also be used as a prelude. Playing time: 2.30. Allegro: trot (142). Playing time: 2.50. La Paix: a stately hymn (tatoo). La Rejouissance: grand entrance march at the walk (120). Playing time: 2.20. Minuet: ceremonial walk (104); could be used as exit. Playing time: 1.55. The *Music for the Royal Fireworks* is most suitable for very ceremonial occasions.

You'll also find very suitable selections in *Water Music*.

Haydn   Symphony no. 88 in G Major. There is lovely trot music (160) in the last movement.

Symphony no. 93 in D Major. First movement: transition to minuet at 1.45 following a slow introduction. Good for trot (156). Second movement: quiet 4/4 meter. Third movement: Minuet; excellent trot music (144). Fourth movement: Allegro; trot (140).

Symphony no. 94 in G Major, *The Surprise*. The minuet is quite lovely for the trot (160).

Symphony no. 101 in D Major, *The Clock*. Marvelous trot music (150) in the minuet. Playing time: 5.30.

Symphony no. 104 in D Major.* Here too we find wonderful trot in minuet (140).

Kreisler   *Old Viennese Dances**

Künneke   *Biedermeier Suite,* opus 53*

Ecosaise. Good trot music (148).

Liszt   Hungarian Rhapsodies nos. 1, 2, 3. For all three pieces, the second halves are very useful, especially for the trot (152–60). They close with a fast, dramatic section that is most appropriate.

Les Préludes. From this truly heroic-sounding music we can use a trot (170), and the last section is wonderfully suitable for a resounding close and imposing final formation.

Mozart   Symphony no. 29 in A Major, K. 201.* Fourth movement: Allegro con Spirito; 3/4 time canter (108); possible for the pas de deux. Playing time: 4.07.

Symphony no. 33 in B-flat Major, K. 319. First movement: Allegro; 3/4 time (56). Fourth movement: Allegro; very lovely, dancelike trot (168); just unfortunate that the closing isn't suitable for the salute. Playing time: 6.50.

Symphony no. 35 in D Major, the *Haffner* Symphony, K. 385. First movement: Allegro; very lovely trot (152). Playing time: 4.27. Third movement: Minuet; possible for very balletlike walk figures (108). Playing time: 3.27. Fourth movement: finale; trot (146). Playing time: 3.54.

Symphony no. 39 in E-flat Major, K. 543. First movement: Allegro; trot (162). Third movement Minuet; very lovely trot (140).

Symphony no. 40 in G Minor, K. 550. First movement: tempo 108, perhaps good for canter. Third movement: Minuet; trot (144–56).

Symphony no. 41 in G Minor, the *Jupiter* Symphony, K. 551. First movement: Allegro; excellent trot (158). Can be used from 0.00 to 6.15. Total playing time: 11.25. Third movement: Minuet; exemplary trot (162). Playing time: 4.20. Fourth movement: Moltò Allegro; possible for canter (120); somewhat too slow? Playing time: 13.06.

Symphony no. 73 in C Major. First movement: walk. Second movement: very dancelike trot (160). Third movement: canter (112). Fourth movement: very rhythmical trot (164).

March in D Major, K. 408.2.* Very good for work at the walk. Also good for pas de deux.

Horn Concerto in D Major, K. 412. The rondo* is especially suitable for canter (88).

Overture to *The Marriage of Figaro*. Good continuous trot music (140). Playing time: 4.15.

Overture to *The Impressario*. Suitable trot (170). Playing time: 4.45.

Overture to *The Abduction from the Seraglio*. Very good beginning, suitable for entrance at the trot (156). Playing time: 1.35.

Overture to *The Magic Flute*. Very good trot music (158) in the first 1.30 as well as the final 3.05.

Serenade from *A Little Night Music*. First movement: Allegro; trot (148). Playing time: 5.15. Third movement: Minuet; dancelike walk (120). Playing time: 2.18. Fourth movement: Rondo; canter (110).

Serenata notturna in D Major, K. 239. First movement: March; entrance at the walk (120). Playing time: 2.56. Second movement: Minuet; gallant, delicate, collected canter (88). Playing time: 4.56. Third movement: Rondo Allegro; canter (98), then trot.

Popy

Suite Orientale. Very well suited for trot and canter.

Ravel

Bolero. A Spanish-Moorish melody with hypnotizing tempo. Sometimes called "the longest crescendo in the world." A very interesting piece that is often played at 110–20, which is too slow for the trot and too fast for the canter. Try to find a recording with a more suitable tempo. Playing time: 18.10.

Schubert

Symphony no. 6 in C Major, D. 589. Last movement: very balletlike walk music ending with a trot (148).

Overture in the Italian Style. From the middle section through till the end we find very useful trot music (144) with a canter finale.

Tchaikovsky

Capriccio italien, op. 45. Brilliant introductory fanfare; from about 6 minutes till the end at 14.10, we find very suitable trot and canter music. There is one grand trot tarantella (150) and a very good finale!

Polonaise from *Eugene Onegin.* Excellent canter music that could also be used as a canter entrance. Playing time: 4.44.

BALLET MUSIC

Adam

Music from *Giselle.* First Act; Part 1: Only the ending is very useful; trot and canter from about 17.00 to 21.00. Part 2: Can be used from 2.50 to 6.45. Act 2: Here we find some really superbly suitable sections.

Bayer, Joseph

The Fairy Doll. Ballet in one act with twenty individual scenes. Mainly it is the last sections, specifically scenes fifteen through twenty that are quite useful. This is well suited for young riders.

Beethoven

The Creatures of Prometheus. An interesting work. Powerful symphonic music.

Music for a Horse Ballet. Different scenes connected by a repeating, dancelike rondo. Good for all gaits.

Borodin

Prince Igor. The *Polovtzian Dances* are well suited for canter (100). Playing time: 10.36.

Delibes

Sylvia. Dance of the Huntresses for trot and canter; slow swinging waltz for slow trot (150).

Donizetti

La Favorite, Second Act. The *Ceremonial Dances* provide glorious, very useful music.

Glinka	*A Life for the Czar.* Polonaise and Mazurka. Very lovely dance melodies.
Gounod	*Faust.* As tempting as this music is, only the *Faust Waltzes* from the first scene are good to ride to. The second from the last (sixth) is very good, and the last (seventh) is useful for the trot.
Hellmesberger	Suite from *The Pearls of Iberia.* Light, sprightly operetta music à la Offenbach. Would make a gay quadrille.
Khachaturian	Symphonic suite from the ballet *Gayane.* Rhythmical, dynamic music for all gaits.
Lortzing	*Casanova.* Good music; flows lightly along.
	Undine. Folksy, melodic, suitable music.
	Zar und Zimmermann. The *Wooden Shoe Dance* is a rhythmical, hammering trot melody (176).
Massenet	*The Cid.* Useful music, especially the last section.
Mozart	*Idomeneo.* The composer created for this opera colossal symphonic ballet music, much of which is very useful.
Paisello	*Proserpine.* Part 1: trot (152); Part 2: canter (72); Part 3: walk; Part 4: canter (95) or trot (190).
Ponchielli	*La Gioconda. Dance of the Hours* is excellent music, beginning with a trot (136), and crescendoing to (160). Finale is a canter (92).
	Cinderella. In places quite useful. Music is in the style of modern classical, similar to Ravel and Mussorgsky.
Respighi	*The Magic Shop.** Ballet with many interesting, but often too short, individual scenes. The first half is the most useful. The fifth scene is a sassy, lighthearted scene with dissonant trumpets.
Rossini	Ballet suite from *The King of Gourmets.* Modern sound; very suitable in parts.
Rubinstein	*Feramors.** Ballet music and wedding procession

are suitable for all gaits. Wedding procession: trot (160); canter (96).

Schubert

Rosamunde. Ballet music no. 2: quiet canter (94). Playing time: 5.30.

Strauss, Johann, Jr.

Fledermaus Quadrille. Well-known melodies from *Die Fledermaus.* Choreographed as a Fasching's quadrille.

Knight Pazman. Part 1: walk entrance (104), followed by trot (160); Parts 2 and 3: Waltz and Czardas; not suitable.

Viennese Carnival Quadrille, op. 124. Six musical numbers for walk, trot, and canter. Joyous, sprightly.

Tchaikovsky

The Nutcracker.* Overture: walk (112); *March*: trot (150); *Dance of the Sugar Plum Fairies*: 3/4 time (68), *Flute Dance*: trot (144); *Trepak*: trot (170); *Waltz of the Flowers*: canter (64); closing waltz: canter (72).

Swan Lake. Useful are waltzes: trot and canter (68–80); *Dance of the Swans*: trot (168); *Hungarian Dance*: walk and trot (176).

Verdi

The Four Seasons from *Sicilian Vespers.* Gradiose, four-part ballet, brilliantly instrumented and superbly suitable for a Pas de Quatre.
1. *Winter.* Not much here is useful.
2. *Spring.* A delicate, graceful 3/4 melody for trot (144) from about 3.35; good close for canter (96).
3. *Summer.* Useful 3/4 melody for trot (140) from about 3.00 till 5.00.
4. *Fall.* Very suitable. Trot (160 and 168) and canter (100).

Aida. Dance of the Moors: lovely, very exotic music for trot (160), unfortunately only 1.25 long. *Triumphal March*: well-known stately walk march. Playing time: 1.25. Ballet music: very good, exotic, inspiring trot music (160). Playing time: 4.00.

Macbeth. Ballet music from the third act is only partially useful.

Otello. Begins with an interesting tone mixture of flutes and percussion; good for walk (112). Playing time: 1.30. Following a quiet middle section, concludes with trot.

Il Trovatore, third act. Ballet music with a playing time of 25 minutes. Suitable to very good; unfortunately, individual elements are somewhat short.

Weber

Invitation to the Dance. Glorious melody in 3/4 time; ideal music for the canter if it's not played too slowly.

Winkler

Ballet in the old style from *The Prince of Monterosso*, some of which is quite useful.

MUSIC FOR THE INDIVIDUAL KUR THROUGH PAS DE QUATRE

Until now, the quadrille has been the focus of our discussion. I would like to emphasize, however, that all of the preceding chapters are equally applicable to riding in smaller groups, for the pas de deux, pas de droit and pas de quatre (see figure 5). I have drawn up a particular selection of music for these small groups simply because there is so much, especially from the genre of chamber music. Divertimenti, serenades, and dances whose special character and orchestration make them less suitable for the full quadrille are quite appropriate for the presentation of small groups.

Auber

Overture to *The Black Domino.* Very interesting trot (160–68) and canter (90–115). Playing time: 8.12.

Bach, Johann Sebastian

Brandenburg Concerto no. 2 in F Major. First movement: trot (168).

Brandenburg Concerto no. 3 in G Major. First movement: trot (160).

Berlioz

La Damnation de Faust. Dance of the Will-o-the-Wisps and *Dance of the Sylphs*: trot (148).

Brahms

Hungarian Dances no. 5 and no. 6.

Delibes

Ballet music from *Sylvia*. See "Ballet Music."

Handel

Concerto grosso in D Major, op. 6, no. 10. Final movement: Gallant, melodic trot (160).

Hummel

Introduction, *Theme and Variations for Oboe and Orchestra*, op. 102. The *Theme* and to a certain extent the *Variations* are quite useful.

Mozart

This composer wrote quite a lot that is ideal for ceremonial occasions and for a public knowledgeable about both riding and music.

Ballet music from *Les Petits Riens*, K. 299b, postscript 10. Majestic, gripping, dancing melodies with a hint of erotic charm. Given a little bit of feel with two charming and musically talented riders, one should be able to create quite a gem with this one.

The same goes for:
A Little Night Music, K. 525 (see under "Symphonic Music")
Serenata notturna, K. 239 (see under "Symphonic Music")
Divertimento in D Major no. 11. Useful here are the Allegro Molto and the Minuet.

March in D Major, K. 408.2. Walking march (118).

Haffner Serenade in D Major, K. 250. First movement: walk; seventh movement: Minuet; trot; eighth movement: Allegro Assai; canter.

Ponchielli

Ballet music to *La Gioconda, Dance of the Hours*: trot (160) and canter (92).

Rossini

This composer wrote several string sonatas in his early years. Riders with a sense for music should explore these *sonate a quattro*.

Sonata no. 1 in G Major. Moderato: trot (140). Playing time: 3.20. Andantino: a beautiful melody, but too slow with its 128 temp. Allegro: canter (92). Playing time: 2.35.

Sonata no. 2 not very good to ride to.

Sonata no. 3 in C Major. Use here the melodic and beautiful Moderato: trot (160–68). Playing time: 2.30.

Sonata no. 4 in B Major. Allegro Vivace: trot (152). Andantino: not suitable. Allegretto: a real gem for the pas de deux at the trot (170).

Schubert	*Ballet music II* from *Rosamunde*: canter (94). Playing time: 5.32.
	Five German Dances, D. 90. Some parts can be worked with well.
Suppé	Overture to *Poet and Peasant*. With some editing, this overture could be very interesting to work with.
Tchaikovsky	Ballet music from *The Nutcracker*. See under "Ballet Music."

GENERAL SUGGESTIONS

In looking for music to ride to, focus on the following composers:

Adolphe Adam, Daniel-François-Esprit Auber, Gaetano Donizetti, Charles Gounod, Jacques Offenbach, Gioachino Rossini, Franz von Suppé, Johann Strauss, Sr., Johann Strauss, Jr., Josef Strauss.

Further, pay particular attention to those sections in the works titled:

Allegro, Allegro Vivace, Gavotte, Mazurka, Minuet, Polonaise, Polka, Tarantella.

In these sections there is almost always something useful to be found.

Figure 5
Perfect harmony in the pas de deux. Josef Neckermann on Mariano and Harry Boldt on Remus, 1965. (Photo: W. Menzendorf)

PART II

THE QUADRILLE

IN COMPETITION

CHAPTER EIGHT

Organizing
a Quadrille Competition

INTRODUCTION
TO QUADRILLE COMPETITIONS

The ridden quadrille has enjoyed increasing popularity in recent years, awakening in many a rider or riding teacher the desire to match their productions to those of others in open competition. As the individual and the pairs kur to music have made for themselves a permanent niche in the competition world, now the quadrille is beginning to develop a new chapter in equine sports.

This development has presented horse show organizers and, above all, the judges with new tasks. In some places quadrille competitions are already being held to the complete satisfaction of all involved. For example, in Germany at the Hanoverian State Association, a "Task Force for Quadrille Competitions" has been in existence for several years. Riding club officials, judges, and quadrille directors have worked to draw up guidelines and criteria for judging the quadrille. These have been used very successfully. It is particularly welcome that a team of judges has formed who are especially interested in the quadrille and who are already judging these competitions.

What marks the difference between quadrille and other team competitions are the two extra criteria of artistic performance (kur) and music that must be judged individually and then in combination with the technical quality of the riding (see figures 6 and 7 on page 57).

The growing popularity of quadrille competitions among riders and audiences cannot be overlooked. In Hamburg, Training and First Level quadrille tournaments have been held locally each year since 1978. On a single day up to nineteen quadrille teams have made presentations. For years a similar competition has been held as an indoor show in Münster, Germany. On a single evening, up to 4,000 spectators have filled the arena for this occasion.

PLANNING
THE QUADRILLE COMPETITION

The Date

In setting the date for the competition, it is important to keep in mind that, given one or two practice sessions per week, a quadrille will need at least four weeks practice time prior to the show to work out the last details. For this reason, the competition should not be scheduled immediately following vacation times when people will have been off on trips. The summer horse show season has also proven impractical. October through November, then, seems an ideal time for the quadrille competition. The weeks just before Christmas are also a possibility, although in winter it will be important to offer all participants indoor stabling for their horses and it would be equally necessary to have a second indoor arena for warm-up.

During this initial planning, select which groups will be invited to participate and send out invitations enough in advance so that they can begin to practice in earnest and won't have to settle for last-minute improvizations.

Regulations and Scope of the Competition

Kur or compulsory test? In planning quadrille competitions, the question always arises as to whether it should be held as a compulsory test, or to require both kur and compulsory tests. Let me dissuade you from the latter. Just from the standpoint of time, two tests are too many. Training and First Level riders are going to be relieved to get just one test over with. A second First Level test that would have to be memorized would pose quite a burden.

Think, too, of the quadrille director who might have both a junior and a senior quadrille group to coach and who, with the double test requirement, would have to get through a total of four presentations, two of which might have to have been memorized.

Freedom of artistic expression is the cornerstone of the quadrille. Thus, a compulsory test wouldn't really be a quadrille any more, as it would leave no room for choreography or the development of an idea. A "compulsory quadrille" would be nothing more than a team competition to the accompaniment of music. Judges would be limited to assessing the turnout and the level of riding.

The compulsory movements and figures to be built in are taken

Figure 6

A happy-go-lucky pony quadrille from the riding club in Berlin-Lichtenrade. (Photo: W. Menzendorf)

Figure 7

Welsh pony stallions in a sulky quadrille presented by the St. George's Riding and Driving Club, Alpen/Niederrhein, West Germany. (Photo: W. Menzendorf)

directly from the official test rides prescribed for various levels and must
be stated explicitly in the description.

Due to the amount of work connected with the quadrille competition,
it would be unwise to try to combine this with other kinds of tests. Perhaps it would be possible to follow the quadrille competition with some
classes over fences for which the quadrille horses would qualify.

Categories

It should be clear that the first attempt to stage a quadrille competition should be local and just for Training and First Level. Later, in expand-
ing the scope of the show, Second Level can be added. This will encourage
the participation of more advanced dressage riders and will elevate the
level of the competition. There won't be much demand for the Third or
Fourth Level quadrille in competition.

Figure and Movements at the Individual Levels

Training Level: Working walk, trot, canter; the 20-meter circle;
changes of rein through the diagonal, short diagonal,
and from the center line.

First Level: Working walk, trot, canter; lengthen stride at walk,
trot, canter; 20- and 10-meter circles; leg yield;
shoulder-in.

Second Level: Working walk, trot, canter; lengthen stride, all gaits;
collected trot; medium and collected canter;
medium walk; travers; countercanter; half turn on
the haunches.

The halt should not be required in Training through Second Level,
nor should turns from the halt, because the quadrille lives through movement. If, however, someone has been able to build in the halt harmoniously, then this shouldn't be marked negatively.

Figures ridden that are of a higher level than appropriate for each
level should not be scored. Required figures left out must result in points
being deducted.

Work at the walk should last no longer than two minutes in total; but
here too, a good choreography should be the final standard.

From First Level, the quadrille should be memorized or ridden to
whistle signals, although these should not be given by whistling through
one's fingers.

Lastly, the quadrille director shouldn't be giving instructions during the initial or closing salute as these parts belong intrinsically to the quad-rille performance.

Age groups

Childen, juniors, and senior riders should be judged in separate classes. Rules governing exceptions and the substitution of riders and horses will need to be established.

SAMPLE DESCRIPTION: Senior Quadrille:
Open to all riders; however, must be composed of at least 50% senior riders.

Here I would allow the participation of junior riders, but not children. Even when the audience finds it "cute," a twelve-year-old does not belong in a "Senior" Quadrille. This, however, must be explicit in the governing show regulations.

It would be best to divide the classes as follows:

Training Level: Seniors, Juniors, Children
First Level: Seniors, Juniors
Second Level: Seniors, or all qualified riders

Size of Quadrille

Training and First Level quadrilles should be choreographed for eight horses. By allowing upwards of eight horses, we would be making things quite difficult for the judge. It would be like asking him to judge individual riders and a pairs class at the same time.

I would restrict Second Level to four riders as most clubs won't be in a position to put together more Second Level riders or mounts.

Substitute Riders or Horses

Allow two of each for Training and First Levels and one each for Second Level. It is often written into the rules that a rider is allowed to start in only one quadrille. This should perhaps be waived for Second Level in order to ensure enough rides. This would be especially important for shows where the Second Level is being offered for the first time.

Length of Ride

A minimum of ten minutes and a maximum of fifteen has proven quite useful. In the interest of allowing full play of artistic creation, one shouldn't be picky about seconds. A tolerance overrun of about fifteen seconds should be allowed.

Bitting

For Training and First Levels: snaffle bridle. Side reins are allowed at Training Level. For Second Level: double bridle. Bitting must match within the group.

Dress

This determination is not easy to make. The LPO regulations should perhaps be modified, yet one shouldn't lose sight of the classical requirements entirely. Training Level: hunt cap is a must; First Level: seniors could perhaps wear derbies; Second Level and above: top hat.

Top hats should be absolutely forbidden for Training and First Levels. I have read programs where it stated: "Training Level: Derby or Top Hat, Side Reins allowed." If we don't wish to appear very foolish, we can't allow this sort of thing to happen.

I have seen First Level quadrilles ridden in top hats with double bridle where the riders had genuine difficulty staying in the saddle. I have also experienced quadrilles ridden with double bridle where snaffle was required, and another case where a Training Level quadrille was ridden in top hats, where hunt caps or derbies were appropriate. In none of these cases were the groups disqualified. They were allowed to start and in the case of the last example, took home first place.

Organizers, and above all the judges, should have the courage to disqualify groups whose costume and tack does not follow the rules. Thus the rules set forth by the LPO for "dress" and "tack" should be kept in mind, not merely in drawing up the regulations; these should be adhered to also in practice.

It is simply not good style to allow a quadrille group that hasn't followed the regulations to take part, and then, because they were the only entry for that class, to go home with the blue. This sort of experience leaves a bad taste in the mouths of those who do follow the rules. We can't afford to build the quadrille as a new form of competition on such a basis.

Spoken Command or Whistle

In the discussion of whether a quadrille should be memorized, or ridden to spoken command or whistle signals, I would like to put forth a few ideas for consideration. Training Level quadrilles, and perhaps even some at First Level, should be ridden to some sort of command. Especially for the first public appearances this will probably be necessary.

Should the commands be carried out as full commands, as in a lesson, (for example, "File, working trot rising!"; "Twenty-meter circle at C"), or should they be shortened to a single cue word, such as "Circle," "Trot," "Diagonal"? In my opinion, this short signal is the best solution, except in situations where a figure is to be performed by the entire group at the same time. Here I would use, for example, "Volté, march!" or "Turn left, march!"

If the class is announced requiring that the ride be memorized with whistle signal allowed, I would use the whistle as little as possible, for example, only to signal those figures that are to be ridden simultaneously by the entire group. It seems obvious that the signals should not be given by whistling through one's fingers.

Ideally, of course, the quadrille should be ridden without spoken or whistle command, but this requires a great deal of experience on the part of the riders, well-trained horses, and a lot of practice.

Opinions on spoken command and whistle signals are very divided. One rider finds the spoken command too militaristic—reminiscent of other eras: Prussian subjects and imperial courts. Others are disturbed by the whistle that smacks too much of the soccer field and team sports. Still others feel that riding to a whistle signal is about the most primitive thing imaginable! The whistle would most certainly ruin any sense of ceremony, for example, in a pas de quatre done to a Haydn minuet.

One interesting opinion is based on the fact that the Master of Ceremonies used to give spoken commands to lead the classical quadrille dance. This spoken command in French then would seem as integral to the quadrille as its music. The spoken command is also part of the procedure in large military ceremonies (such as the tatoo). Thus, it is argued, the command in French could be added to the ridden quadrille: circle (volter), diagonal (changer), turn (turner), moulinet, echelons, and so forth.

Having studied all these arguments, I have personally come to the following conclusion:

1. Training Level: ridden to spoken command. First Level: ridden to command or memorized. Second Level and above: the ride should be memorized.

2. Spoken commands should be kept to a minimum in order to avoid ruining the atmosphere with constant yelling.

3. Where the ride is memorized, figures to be executed by the whole group at once could be announced by the word, "March!" Not "Volté, March!" or "Left, March!" but simply, "March!"

All individual organizers and associations who have the ultimate responsibility for establishing regulations for such a competition will have to give these items some thought. There should, at any rate, be a single set of regulations governing the rides within a given class.

Judging

In addition to the usual information on judging, there should also be information about the criteria according to which the riding, the music, and the choreography will be judged. If a score sheet is to be used for the competition, a copy of this should be included in the prize list.

Indeed, all the points we have discussed here should be included in the prize list:

> Category
> Levels with Required Movements and Figures
> Age Groups
> Numbers of Horses (if horses or ponies)
> Length of Performance (maximum and minimum)
> Tack Standards
> Dress Standards
> Command or Memorized
> Judging Criteria with Score Sheet

CHAPTER NINE

Holding
a Quadrille Competition

JUDGING CRITERIA
AND SCORE SHEET

The establishment of judging criteria is one of the organizer's most important considerations. The organizer should discuss these standards with the judges in advance in order to arrive at a consensus. I would like to introduce here the scoring sheet developed by the Task Force for Quadrille Competition in Hamburg, which has been used quite successfully.

According to these guidelines, the quadrille is judged according to the following criteria:

I. *Criterion: Artistic Quality*

> Here the emphasis is on the total picture, the music, and the choreography. Points awarded here are then multiplied by a given coefficient. The coefficient of 2 has seemed to work well.

II. *Criterion: Technical Quality*

> Here the focus is on those factors normally judged in any dressage test of a given level.

III. *Penalty Points:*

> Established rules for the deduction of points enable the judge to work with a clear conscience and help to increase the point spread. For example, if a horse leaves the arena, which in a dressage test would result in disqualification, points should be deducted in the quadrille competition. This would allow an otherwise well-ridden quadrille to proceed, but the penalty points would prevent this group from taking first place.

Horse Show held on: _____   Team: _____

at: _____

Class Number: _____   Director: _____

I. CONTENT: Artistic Impression

	Score	Comments
1. Showmanship of Team and Director (Turnout and Match of Horses)		
2. Choreographic Composition (Richness of Ideas, Variety, and Originality)		
3. Difficulty of Movements, Figures, and Sequences		
4. Appropriateness of Music and Suitability to Movement and Figures (Coordination and Rhythm)		
5. Brilliance		
6. Harmony and Relationship of Movements to the Music		
SUM PART I:		
Coefficient = x 2: (unless otherwise specified)		

II. PRESENTATION: Technical Execution

	Score	Comments
7. Salute Formations Entrance: _____ Exit: _____ SUM: _____ × 2 =		
8. Walk (Purity)		
9. Trot		
10. Canter		
11. Impulsion		
12. Suppleness, Fluidity, Obedience and, from Second Level, Collection		
13. Seat and Effectiveness of Rider		
14. Correctness of Figures (Track, Letter Markers, Distances and Overall Discipline)		
SUM PART II:		
SUM PART I:		
SUM PARTS I & II:		
Minus Points Deducted — PART III:		

FINAL SCORE: _____

10 excellent	7 fairly good	4 deficient	1 very poor
9 very good	6 fair	3 fairly poor	0 not shown
8 good	5 satisfactory	2 poor	

PART III: DEDUCTIONS

		Score	Comments
1. Exceeding Time Limit	minus 2 points		
2. Use of Side Reins or Martingales (each)	_____ x 3		
3. Leaving the Arena	_____ x 3		
4. Off Course (each occurance)	_____ x 6		
5. Necessary Regrouping	_____ x 14		
6. Fall from Horse	_____ x 4		
7. Other Disruptive Factors (Deduction Commensurate with Severity)	_____		
SUM PART III:			

Date: _____

Signature of Judge(s) _____

_____

Quadrille Team: _____

Director: _____

I.   (1) Turnout

     (2) Creativity

     (3) Difficulty

     (4) Music

     (5) Originality

     (6) Harmony

II. (7) Salute Formations

     (8) Walk

     (9) Trot

     (10) Canter

     (11) Impulsion

     (12) Obedience of Horses

     (13) Seat & Influence of Rider

     (14) School Figures

FIRST LEVEL	shown	score
Walk Working Trot Lengthening at Trot Working Canter		

SECOND LEVEL	shown	score
Working Trot Medium Trot Collected Trot Working Canter Medium Canter Collected Canter Countercanter Canter Volté		

Points must be deducted from final score for required figures and movements not shown.

As one can see from the score sheet, the artistic criterion is to be given particular emphasis through the use of a coefficient factor. Exact standards and expectations are established here through the many individual criteria (see page 64).

Judges should note in their scoring that the initial formation to salute does not have to be done at the halt. The groups we pattern our efforts after, such as the Spanish Riding School, salute while moving down the center line. Thus the salute done in motion should be accepted and the salute done at the canter should perhaps even be awarded plus points (see illustration 8).

For establishing judging criteria for the quadrille competition well-known judges have provided us with a wealth of helpful tips in their discussions regarding judging of the individual kur or team freestyle. Dietmar Specht has dealt with the topic, "The Judging of the Team Dressage Kur" in depth in an article written for the "Mitteilung der Deutschen Richtervereinigung" of December, 1983.

It is important that the judges familiarize themselves with the task prior to the competition. The judges should also have thought through the points discussed in this book. It would help, of course, if they were also well versed in music.

Figure 8
Quadrille Championships in Hamburg, 1984. Arrowhead formation down center line. The Riding Club at Bredenbeker Teich, Hamburg.
(Photo: D. Theinert)

It has worked well for us in practice to hold two classes simultaneously, alternating between the two groups, juniors and seniors for example. Each group is assigned to a separate team of judges. This gives each team of judges time to complete the work of assessment while the next quadrille can get started. This arrangement also holds the interest of the audience better.

To help the judges, a checklist of all required movements should be included on the score sheet, especially from First Level onward (see page 65).

Finally, ponies and horses should always be judged in separate classes.

THE ARENA

The arena in which the test will take place should, of course, measure the official 20 × 40 meters. The footing should also correspond to LPO requirements. This also applies to the letter markings and the border marks. The judges will sit, as usual, at C; entrance is at A, which allows the group riding in to enter on the center line.

In addition to the arena where the test is to take place, there must be a second area with the same measurements to allow for practice. An area for individual first warmups should also be provided.

THE SOUND SYSTEM

Music is a very critical element to the success of the quadrille. This is true also of the quality of the public address system upon which it is played. Unfortunately in this respect, the criterion "Music" is often neglected. The quadrille is to be a musical experience. Music and the ridden figures are to merge into a unity. For this to happen, the PA system must be of good quality.

The music industry today produces tapes of the very best sound quality, and the quadrille director will look for the best in order to get good quality sound reproduction. How disappointing to find that all these efforts have been in vain due to the poor quality of the system used at the show.

For good quality sound reproduction, a system must at least allow the volume to be regulated and have separate tone controls for treble and bass. It is very helpful if it also has a speed control. The person operating the system must be able to turn off the local speakers so that the volume in the arena can be checked. Arena speakers should be mounted to allow both the public and participants to hear well. The rider needs to hear his music both as an inspiration and for the all-important cues to the figures. When he can't hear the music, which in quadrilles ridden without command is the signal for starts, figures, and transitions, he is going to feel lost indeed. Because the music is of paramount importance to the success of the quadrille, organizers of the competition must pay special attention to the quality of its reproduction.

I was once able to see a commercially made videotape of the individual kur at the world championships in Lucerne. The acoustics were so indescribably awful that even the best-known melodies, such as *The Blue Danube Waltz*, were hardly recognizable. This probably came about because music coming from all the different speakers on the field set at various distances reached the microphone at different intervals, creating a kind of echo effect. Those who aspire to make this kind of film should do a little brushing up on physics and photography. Above all they should know the speed of sound. This means that the sound from two speakers that are set at different distances from the microphone, for example 330 meters and 165 meters away, will reach the microphone with a difference of half a second. You can imagine what a cacophony would result from four speakers being set at various distances.

An organizer will have to explore these points in order to provide optimal listening quality, both for the riders and the audience. Quadrille competitions—indeed all tests ridden to music—live by the music and the quality of its reproduction.

Note: In addition to following the regulations governing recognized and nonrecognized shows, the organizer of the quadrille competition should consult local authorities about regulations governing the outdoor use of loudspeakers.

CHAPTER TEN

Recommendations for the Quadrille Director

From my years of experience in working with quadrilles and in showing them in competition, I would like to give the instructors, the quadrille directors, a few suggestions.

PRACTICE SESSIONS

Get a score sheet as soon as possible before the competition so that you can inform yourself as well as your riders what the judging criteria will be. Keep working to improve your riders' seat. Emphasize the importance of swinging gaits. Keep in mind that this is basically a dressage test. Further, the entrance and exit salute must be performed with the same precision as the rest of the figures.

At first keep working on individual figures and passages without music, remembering from time to time to give the hroses a break and a chance to stretch. Most problems, especially in the canter work in pairs, comes from not building in such breaks and from the mistake riders make of hanging on the inside rein.

In choosing your horses, choose ones you can count on, rather than the horse with a lot of movement that could lose its nerve at the wrong time.

I have discovered that tape recorders often play at differing speeds. Having contacted manufacturers, I was told that there is a norm for tape recorders with a tolerance factor of 3 percent allowed for models designed for everyday use. For our purposes this would mean that in a twelve-minute quadrille there might be a difference of up to twenty-one seconds. Let's take the following example. The recorder you use at home to practice with runs 3 percent faster than the norm. The recorder used at the competition runs 3 percent slower than the norm. This results in a difference of forty-two seconds! You can image the difficulty you might run into with the final salute if you don't build some flexibility into your plan.

During practice, point out distinctive sections in the music that are to be matched with specific figures. In this way the riders will be able to tell if they are correct, or running either a little early or late.

Build an alternative figure into the final section of your quadrille. Just before the final salute would be best. In this way, a performance can be lengthened or shortened as necessary. This is especially important if you want your salute to fall exactly on the closing chord of the music.

The other method of reducing these time differences would be to bring along your own recorder and hook it up at the competition.

PRESENTING THE QUADRILLE
AT THE COMPETITION

All tack needs to be checked before the start of your group, especially the bandages. I have seen performances where bandages came loose and participants rode with open jackets and ties flying. Appoint an assistant to check these last-minute details for you, as you will probably be busy with other things.

A second assistant will be needed at the PA system for the music. Establish a hand signal for volume as well as regulation of treble and bass. Your musical assistant can then help to emphasize high points in the quadrille and also beef up sections that are undramatic.

Judges have a good eye for detail. They are pleased to note that the horses' manes are all braided on the same side.* Another possibility would be to braid according to the lineup. Those horses from the middle to M could be braided to the right, those from the middle to H braided to the left.

If a boutonniere is to be worn, it should not be heavy as this could cause it to dangle. Also ladies should try to wear similar hair styles. Of course, these are little things, but they can have a very positive influence on points given for turnout.

The quadrille director should best stand at B or E depending on the direction of the wind and position of the sun. If the quadrille is to be ridden to spoken commands, then these must be given loudly and distinctly.

Translator's Note: In Germany, it is not considered improper to braid on the left. It is usually not done in the United States.

If whistle signals are to be used, these should not be given by whistling through one's fingers. The director should give the commands from memory. Only if he has several quadrille groups to present should he use a note card. At the closing salute, the director should stand either directly in front of the formation or to the right side of it. For this to go smoothly, the director will have to pay particular attention to the timing of the salute.

The question has arisen whether the director should be on foot or mounted. If he is mounted, it needs to be established where he should stand, or if, perhaps, he should even ride at the lead. Several factors should govern this decision. If we are talking about a Training or First Level quadrille group, then the director should be unmounted and stand outside the ring. This is due to the fact that during the training and practice sessions, the director will need to be watching and correcting the riders, which he'll not be able to do mounted. At the competition he should stand out of the way of the group, outside the arena either at E or B.

From Second Level onward, each group could decide this individually. At gala performances of the most famous quadrilles, like the Cadre Noir, the German school quadrille of the Hanoverian Cavalry School, or at the

Figure 9

Pas de quatre. Volté at the trot along the long side. The Riding Club at Bredenbeker Teich, Hamburg, 1984. (Photo: D. Theinert)

Spanish Riding School, the directors ride at the head. Thus if the quadrille director is to be mounted, the level of the quadrille should be high and the director should be an excellent rider.

It goes without saying that a sprightly piece should be chosen for the exit march. The exit can be done at any gait. I would suggest using the walk or trot for Training and First Levels. From Second Level on the canter would also be appropriate.

FINAL OBSERVATIONS

Having reached the end of my discussion, I hope that I have been successful in introducing the reader to the world of the quadrille competition and its music. I hope, too, to have won more friends for this relatively new form of equestrian competition. For the experienced quadrille directors among you, I hope you have found some new musical ideas.

Finally, the dressage kur, either as individual or pairs kur to music, has gained quite a bit in popularity in recent times. In choosing music for this book, I have placed a great deal of emphasis on finding suitable music for the kur as well. I have heard a lot of music used for the kur or freestyle that wasn't very appropriate. Thus, I hope also to have given these riders new musical inspiration.

Most especially though, I wish from the bottom of my heart to have given impetus, in these days where all styles of riding are becoming more and more popular, to nurture the traditions of classical riding, traditions created and molded by such men as Gustav Steinbrecht, Hans von Heydebreckt, Waldemar Seunig, Alois Podhajsky, Felix Bürkner, and Gustav Rau.

I would like to think that we are once again at a crossroads in riding as we were in 1918 and 1945. If the problem then was to reorganize German riding and to begin anew, then today it is to maintain quality and not lose sight of a valuable tradition in face or riding's new popularity.

Standards must be set. The future could lead, as can already be seen today, toward a chaotic cowboylike riding style that is all too often seen in riders of all ages. Even adults tearing about on ponies is no longer an uncommon sight. By this I don't mean to say anything negative about people who just want to let their horses carry them through the woods, instead of walking on their own two feet. I mean nothing against riders who use their horses as a mode of transportation and who derive genuine enjoyment from this.

That vast army of this kind of "bush" rider or Sunday hacker probably counts in the tens of thousands today. These are mostly passionate riders who love their horses. However, this kind of riding has very little relationship to riding in the classical sense of the quadrille toward which we are aiming. Would you find the sight of an overweight adult mounted on a pony a very aesthetic picture?

The other path that riding could take leads in the direction of harmony and beauty, towards the furtherance of classical riding. Even if we never achieve perfection, we should keep striving towards its established ideals (see figure 9). This classical tradition can be fostered especially through the art of the quadrille. In this vein, we must prevent the quadrille in competition from developing in the "negative" direction where it would deteriorate into a kind of clowns' act.

Let us nurture this art, too, with lovely music. Let us take joy again and again in this ballet of horse and rider, a dance of great culture, of harnessed power, a play of figures that defies gravity, a true mirror of the spirit of classical riding as an art.

PART III

PHILOSOPHICAL

OBSERVATIONS

ON RIDING

TO MUSIC

CHAPTER ELEVEN

How Music Affects
the Rider

INTRODUCTION

Having spent many years teaching riding with an emphasis on quadrille work, I find myself pondering ideas that go beyond riding craftsmanship or the musical technicalities necessary for the quadrille. The classical ballet is my inner prototype for the quadrille, because it depicts danced music, music translated into motion.

And, at some point the question posed itself: How does music affect the rider? In pondering the answer, I have had to consider the theory of motion, rhythm, the history of music, and musical therapy. And in attempting an answer here, I have drawn from my own experiences and reflections from my childhood.

In middle school, we had chorus from 1:00 to 2:00 in the afternoon. Our music teacher, Mr. Reichelt, a musician through and through, taught us music from A to Z; from do, re, mi to four-part harmony; from rousing, zesty marching songs to clear, pure Christmas hymns. One day as music class was being dismissed the whole group of us stormed down the stairs singing jubilantly, at the top of our voices, "Daughter of Zion, joy unto you!" To this day, when I recall that scene, I feel the self-same carefree, joyous feeling of that moment. Summing up that boyhood experience today, I would say that our voices had become the instruments of our souls.

I recall having a similar feeling as we put our instruments away in their cases following our weekly school orchestra practice. The melodies of what we had been practicing echoed long in our subconscious. I still recall so well the themes of the *Farewell* Symphony by Haydn or Hindemith's *Wir bauen eine neue Stadt.*

Also, at home on Sunday mornings, my brother—who played clarinet and tenor trumpet—and I—who played violin and a little clarinet—would put a recording on the old handcranked gramophone. For example, we'd choose the march *Free*. We liked this march particularly well because it was the regimental march of the Infantry Regiment Batallion #134 stationed in our town of Plauen/Vogtland. We'd play along to the record on our instruments—more loudly than beautifully. It was our way of letting go musically, and we did it with all our hearts.

It is hard to say whether this ardor was simply typical of adolescence and our growing sense of self-importance; however, common to all these experiences was a state of true euphoria called forth by the music. The recent past holds similar memories. I have that same joyous, carefree, harmonious feeling following a session with a string trio I play with. This state of mind continues through our chat over a glass of wine that typically follows practice, and it is with me still when I go to bed.

At this point, you're probably wondering why I'm telling you all this, and what riding to music has to do with these personal experiences of mine. The answer is that following our quadrille practice sessions, I find an awakening of that same feeling in myself and in my riders.

The quadrille practice is often the best hour I've taught all week, even though it is by far the one that requires the most of me. And I've heard my riders echo these thoughts. (Of course, this doesn't mean that the quadrille practice is always a wild success. I can also be the worst lesson of the week.) It will take a while, just as it does with a group of musicians, to get in tune with one another, to put things together. But when the mental preparation of the riders is complete and that feeling of harmony is found, then the interplay of the ridden figures and the music will all fall into place; the extensions will seem to come of their own accord with the crescendos in the music; the canter will be picked up simultaneously and precisely with the first note of the fortissimo. And when the final salute falls exactly with the last chord of the music, then I see in the faces of my riders an expression I interpret as one of great satisfaction and joy.

This harmonious mood, called forth by the successful completion of a common task, lasts for quite a while; you can hear the riders later while they are untacking in the barn whistling a favorite phrase from "their" quadrille music. The greatest reward for me comes when a rider comes to me afterwards and exclaims from the bottom of his heart, "That was such a marvelous session!" The riders tell me that this inspiration goes home with them as well. And upon hearing "our" Rossini on the radio, they find themselves riding along in their minds.

To the question of how music affects the rider in a quadrille, let's append a second question. Is it really the music that awakens these feelings, or is it instead the working together, the common riding experience?

I rode for many years in team competition and put together quite a few such teams. I know the work entailed in making a team out of a group of riders, and I know the mood awakened by such a team ride. But the difference in the mood of the riders and the director participating in a team ride and those riding in a quadrille I would compare to the happenings at a fancy ball. Imagine such a gala evening: the grand hall, elegant dress, sparkling chandeliers, bubbling champagne, the Vienna Philharmonic playing, couples turning to the strains of the *Emperor's Waltz*. And now picture the whole thing again—*without* music. The dancing couples without the *Emperor's Waltz*—not a single note! It is about as unimaginable as an evening at the ballet without music. There is the same difference between the quadrille and a team ride. Without music it is merely a geometrical play of figures—a purely gymnastic exercise. It is the music that inspires, that causes the soul to swing, to sing. Only through the music will an atmosphere be created that elevates one's whole being.

The rider knows this swinging feeling of relaxation in the moving horse. Even without music he knows what cadence feels like. He knows balance and harmony with his horse. This feeling of moving as one with the horse is the basis of all dressage and must also form the basis of the quadrille. Riding then to just the right inspiring music awakens a feeling of pure joy. The rider becomes a dancer. In the quadrille this inner glow of the rider expands and becomes a shared experience that permeates every corner of the riding hall and can color the atmosphere of an entire show.

HOW MAN IS INFLUENCED BY MUSIC

I'd like to try to explain the mental and spiritual relationships through which man is influenced by music. Man's search for harmony in himself and within his community is a basic drive rooted deeply in all of us. The ancient choral dance is an original expression of this human longing. From this prototype, singing or playing instruments in groups was to develop.

Greek teaching differentiated between constructive and destructive music. According to this ethos, different musical keys and modes unleashed different emotions and behaviors; thus music was regarded as an important pedagogical force. We've certainly all experienced a sense of elation or joy brought about through music. We've also known it to evoke sadness or melancholy. This has been the role music has played as it has accompanied mankind throughout history, in his joy and sorrow, as much in the song of the field laborer as in the resounding trumpeting of a triumphal fanfare.

Various moods and emotions are called forth by the rhythm of the music, by its tempo, and by the melody—that relationship of tones to one another, the intervals, the chords—all of which then create either harmony or disharmony. If only subconsciously, everyone recognizes the cheerful mood of the major keys and the sadness inherent in the minor ones.

We know from physics that tones consist of sound waves. The faster the frequency of these waves, the higher the tone; and the slower the motion, the deeper the tone will be. An experiement conducted by physicist Ernst Chladni (1756–1827) is of great interest to us here. He used a violin bow to cause metal plates strewn with sand or pieces of cork to vibrate and produce various sounds. Depending on the differing qualities of tones and the volume, the sand particles would form specific geometric patterns. Some tones caused the sand to remain unorganized. This phenomenon shows that music (tones) has the ability to cause material elements to move in specific patterns. This, then, parallels Greek ideas on the constructive and destructive qualities of music.[6]

These measurable sound frequencies are picked up by the human ear, but also through the entire outer skin layer, which, of course, is an organ of touch. The brain then translates these senses through complicated processes into commensurate moods.

This is a fairly simple explanation of how music influences man. In addition, however, there are other aspects, some well known, others fairly unresearched, such as the different development of the two halves of the brain, memories stored deep in the subconscious, prenatal musical experiences, and musical training in childhood, as well as the possibilities of reincarnation.

All of these factors produce what we call musicality and explain the difference in influence which music exercises on various individuals. These factors can be grouped in three major categories:

1. Inborn musical talent (heredity)
2. Acquired musical talent through training, study, and practice
3. The talents described above can then be augmented through external forces, that is, through that ethereal harmony described by the Pythagoreans as the "music of the sphere."

Great composers like Bach, Beethoven, Handel, and Mozart had a feel, an antenna for this music of the spheres from which they derived grat creative power.

At this point let's return to riding, riding to music. We have established that the quadrille can bring with it a whole new dimension, an expansion of the mind.

---

6. Rita Jacobs, *Music Therapy* (Bad Liebenzell, West Germany: Four Falkons Press, 1964).

Anyone seriously interested in riding to music needs to peruse the history of music, study the individual epochs and the various musical forms. One should also give thought to the broader ideas that we've focused on in this chapter. From all these sources, a greater understanding of music and its potential relationship to riding will evolve.

Playing music and riding are both rooted in rhythm and tempo. Both require a suppleness of body, an openness of mind, and a harmony of soul. A rider's instrument is his horse. He must bring the horse to swing under him, to exude harmony. At their highest levels of performance, both riding and playing an instrument are art (see figure 10).

Prerequisite to all art though, is the mastery of one's tools. Thus, no matter how deeply involved you are in the musical aspects of this work, it is basic that your practice must first be focused on developing the precision of the figures. In the beginning this must be done without the music. You'll soon notice, however, how positively greedy the riders will be to start working with the music. Only then, when the practice with music can being giving the riders that extra inspiration, can the highest level of performance be attained.

Seen in this way, the quadrille—indeed all riding to music—makes of riding more than a certain technical expertise; the rider contemplates his inner self, examines his relationship with his horse, and from the resulting new awareness grows a more perfect harmony that extends both between the rider and his horse and to his human partners in the quadrille.

Figure 10

Quadrille Championships in Hamburg, 1984. Pas de quatre from the Birkenhof Stables in Stapelfeld, near Hamburg. Pairs diverging at B. (Photo: C. Nagel)

Figure 11

Quadrille Championships in Hamburg, 1984. First Level quadrille showing the volte, to the left and right. The Riding Club at Bredenbeker Teich, Hamburg. (Photo: D. Theinert)

Figure 12

Quadrille Championships, 1984. First Level Quadrille. Awards ceremony. Riding Club at Bredenbeker Teich, Hamburg. (Photo: D. Theinert)

PART IV

THE DRESSAGE ARENA AND BASIC QUADRILLE FIGURES

CHAPTER TWELVE

Basic Figures

Illustrated here are the quadrille figures I have found to be the most useful and expressive. They are depicted for an eight-horse quadrille. Of course, these figures can be infinitely varied and embellished.

In riding the figures, care must be taken to maintain the distances between the riders and to synchronize the figures when riding in two files. The lead riders must maintain constant eye contact with one another, and it is the responsibility of all riders to be alert.

Some figures are particularly suitable for a pas de quatre at the higher levels. See, for example figure 44, "Consecutive Voltés"; figure 46, "Echelon Volté"; figure 49, "The Clover Leaf"; and figure 64, the "Volté in the Corners." At the higher levels these can be ridden at the collected canter and produce very effective figures that dramatically fill the arena space.

In planning the choreography, don't be too exact in figuring the distances. Differences are going to occur anyway, for example those created by the tempo changes within the trot or the canter. In order to even out these time differences, I recommend building in alternate figures. These could be implemented in the transitions from one gait to another or can be very easily added right before the final formation. The circle and the volté are the most useful figures for this. They can be repeated or left out entirely, as necessary.

Prerequisite to all quadrille work is a thorough knowledge of, and ability to perform, the basic lessons of the dressage tests. The director of a quadrille needs to emphasize the importance of riding these school figures exactly (see figures 15–19).

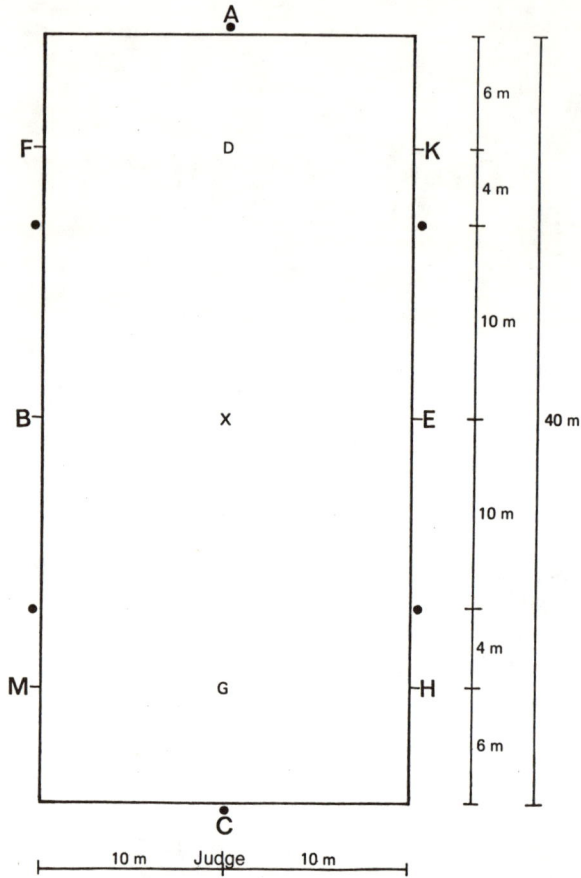

Figure 13: A 20 × 40-meter dressage arena. Designations: Entrance at A. Judge and audience at C. Diagonal markers: M, H, F, K. Circle points: ●.

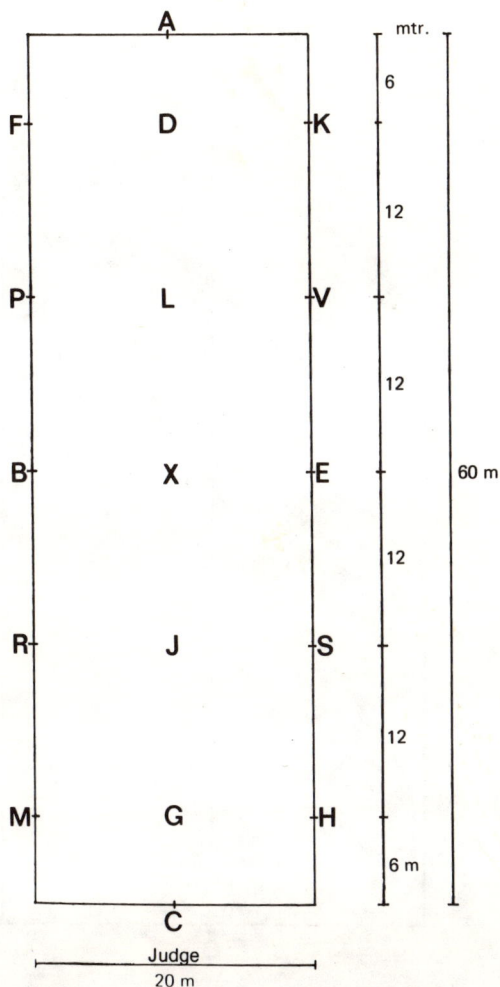

Figure 14: An international 20 × 60-meter dressage arena.

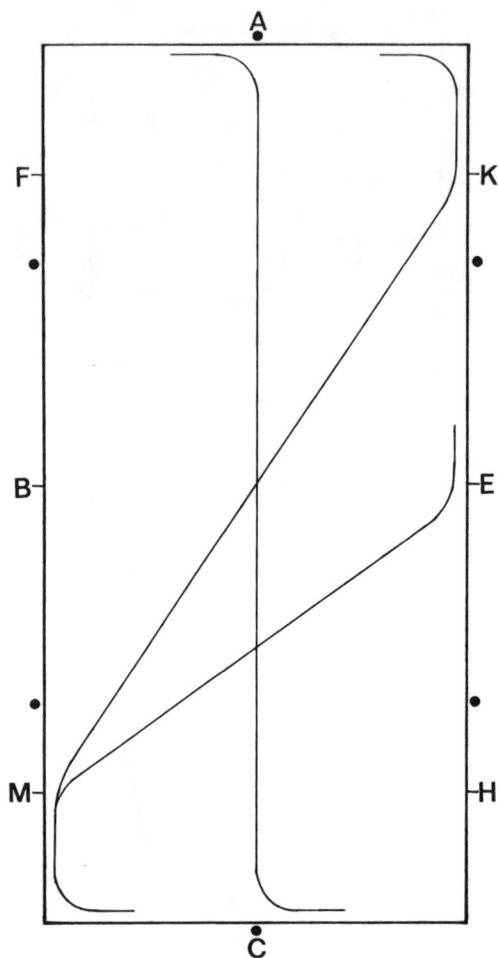

Figure 15: Diagonal lines. A–C is the center line. Note that the change is executed not from the corner, but from the appropriate letter marker.

> A–C: Change rein down the center line.
> M–E: Change rein through the short diagonal.
> M–K: Change rein through the diagonal.

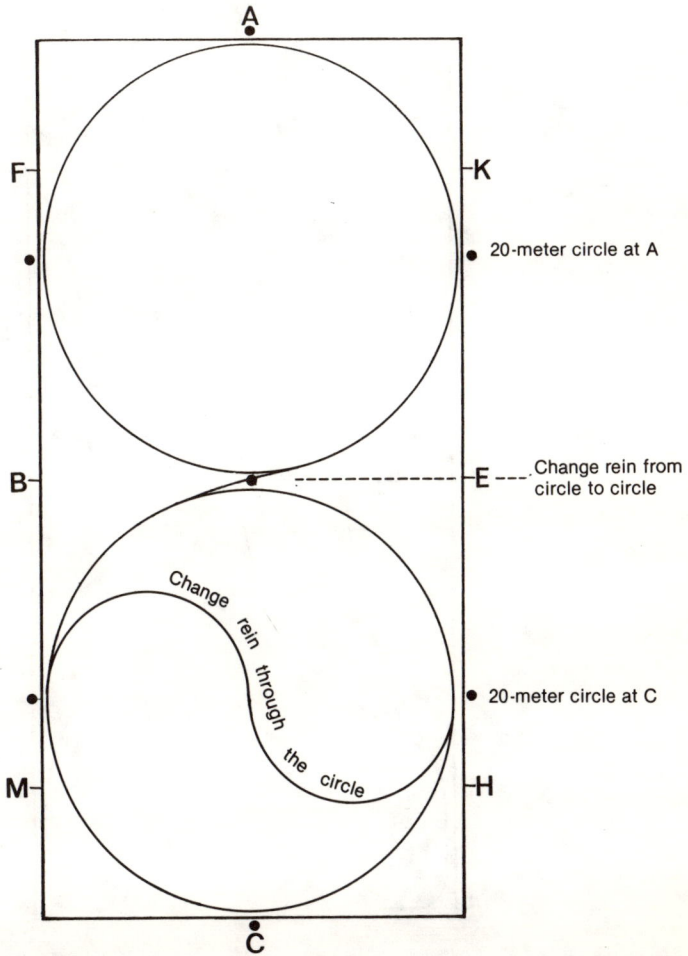

Figure 16: Circle lines. Note: In riding the 20-meter circle, the circle line touches the track at the circle points.

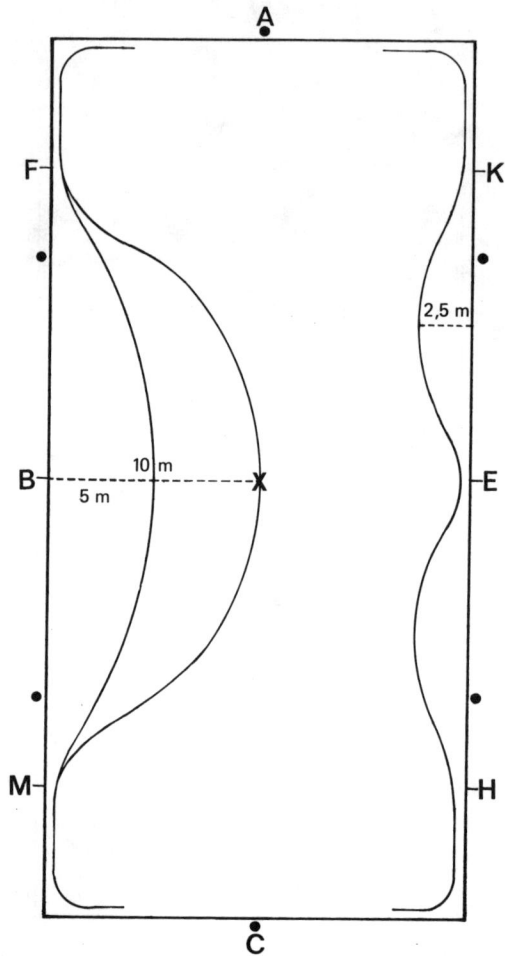

Figure 17: Serpentines along the long side. In normal dressage work the single serpentine should be ridden 5 meters in from the long side; the double serpentine 2.5 meters in. For Training and First Level quadrilles, however, the single serpentine should be ridden to X.

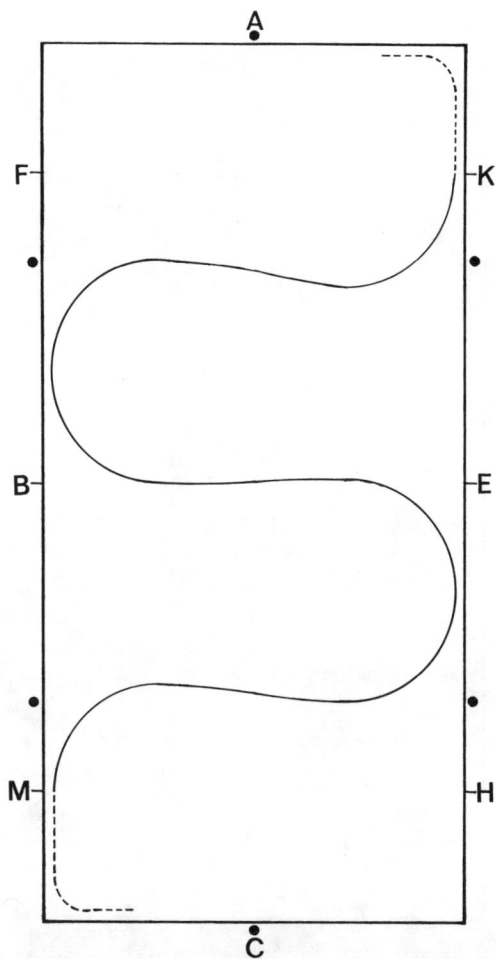

Figure 18: Four loop serpentines, width of the arena, whereby the first and last half-loops are counted. Note that the serpentines begin and end at the diagonal markers (K, F, H, M) and that the loops must come all the way out to the track.

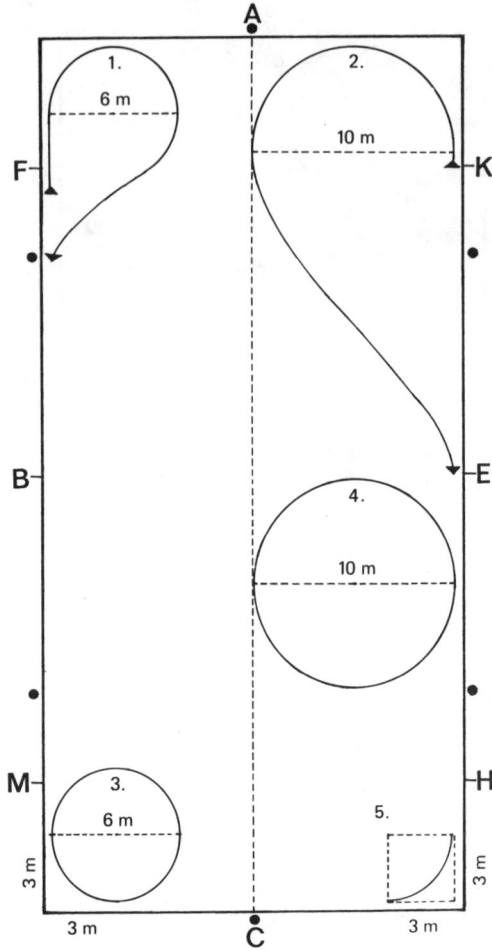

Figure 19: Voltés, the 10-meter circle, and the half-circle and reverse. In Training and First Level quadrilles of eight horses, the volté should be ridden as a 10-meter circle to fill the arena.

1. Half-circle and reverse
2. Half-circle to center line and reverse
3. 6-meter volté
4. 10-meter circle
5. Riding through a corner: same distance as a quarter-volté

CALCULATION OF METERS RIDDEN

The basis for all calculations needed to find a suitable piece of music are the meters ridden in the figures performed in the 20 × 40 dressage arena. The sum of the meters of individual figures is then calculated as total time.

Because these calculations should be kept as simple as possible, we'll measure all figures from one corner to the next. For example, even though the simple serpentine is properly ridden from circle point to circle point, we will calculate the entire distance from the corners. We'll do the same thing for changes through the diagonal.

"Change Rein Through the Diagonal" is calculated as follows:

Diagonal M–K		= 33 meters
plus distance from letter to corner × 2	2 × 6	= 12 meters
Total		= 45 meters

Also we'll be rounding out all calculations to whole meters. For example, the 20-meter circle in a 20 × 40 arena is never ridden all the way to the wall. Thus we'll not calculate 20 × 3.14 (π), but we'll round it out to 20 × 3 = 60 meters. For convenience, I usually round these figures up or down to the nearest multiple of five.

Basic School Figures in Meters

Whole Arena	120 meters
20-Meter Circle	60 meters
10-Meter Circle (also called volté)	30 meters
6-Meter Volté	20 meters
Simple Serpentine to Quarter Line	42 meters
Simple Serpentine to X	45 meters
Double Serpentine	42 meters
Change through Diagonal	45 meters
Change through Short Diagonal	50 meters
Change from Center Line	40 meters

(Again, serpentines and diagonals have been calculated from corner to corner.)

EXAMPLE:

Command	Figure	Meters	Total Meters Ridden
"File, left rein."	File at X facing C X–C	20	20
"At A, circle left, 20 meters, 1½ times."	C–A	60	80
	A–X–A–X	90	170
"At X, circle right, 20 meters, 1½ times."	X–C–X–C	90	260
"At C, go large."	C–corner	10	270
"M–K, change rein."	corner–corner	45	315
"At A, down center line.	corner to A	10	325
Riders 1, 3, 5, 7, volté right;	A–C	40	365
riders 2, 4, 6, 8, volté left."	10-meter volté	30	395

CHANGING METERS TO PLAYING TIME

For figure 20, the following times have been calculated:

Walk	120 meters = 60 seconds	100 meters = 50 seconds
Trot	120 meters = 35 seconds	100 meters = 30 seconds
Canter	120 meters = 25 seconds	100 meters = 20 seconds

If the example cited above is to be ridden at the walk, we would need a suitable piece of music 3 minutes, 18 seconds long.

395 meters × 0.5 seconds = 197.5 seconds = 3 minutes, 18 seconds.

For the trot, we would calculate 395 × 0.3; for the canter 395 × 0.2.

These formulas give a good approximation of the time required. Again, absolutes are impossible to figure due to the variations in horses' speeds. As I have done throughout this book, you can round the figures up or down to the nearest multiple of five to allow for such differences.

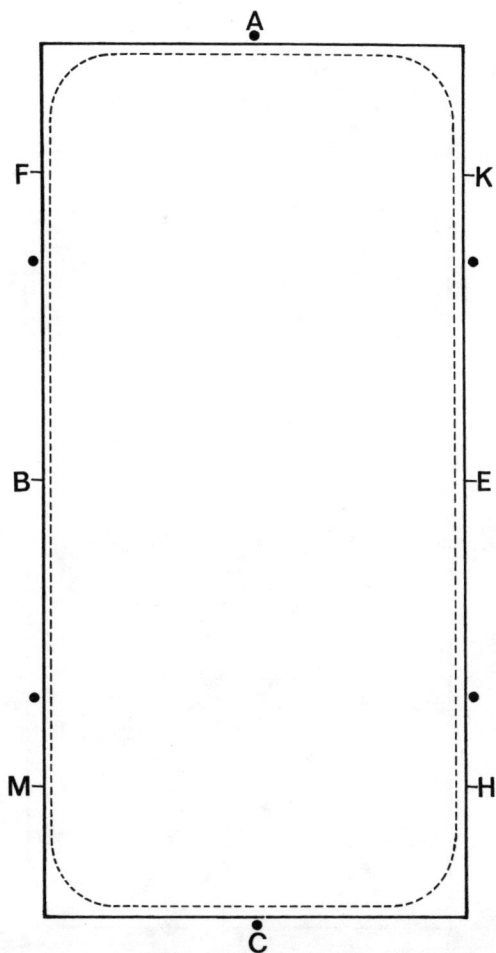

Figure 20: Whole Arena (once around = 120 meters)

Walk = 60 seconds
Trot = 35 seconds
Canter = 25 seconds

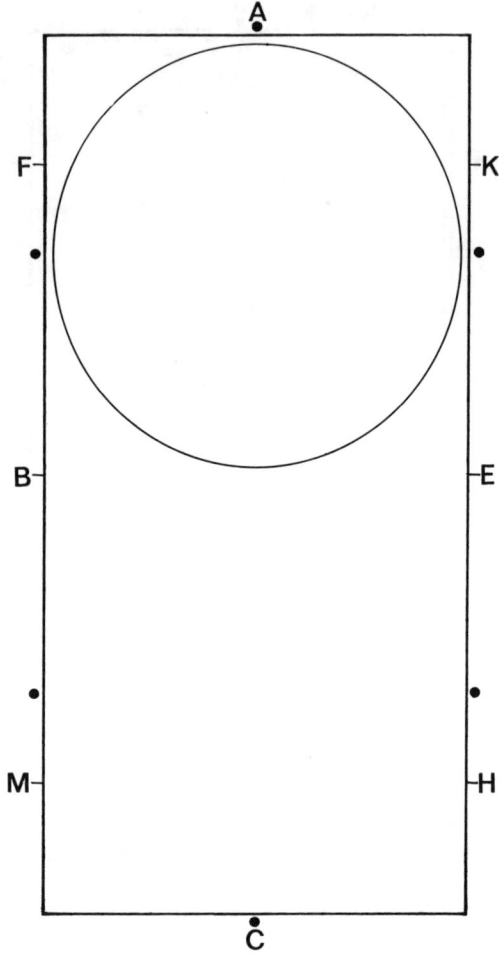

Figure 21: 20-Meter Circle (once around = 60 meters)

Walk = 30 seconds
Trot = 20 seconds
Canter = 15 seconds

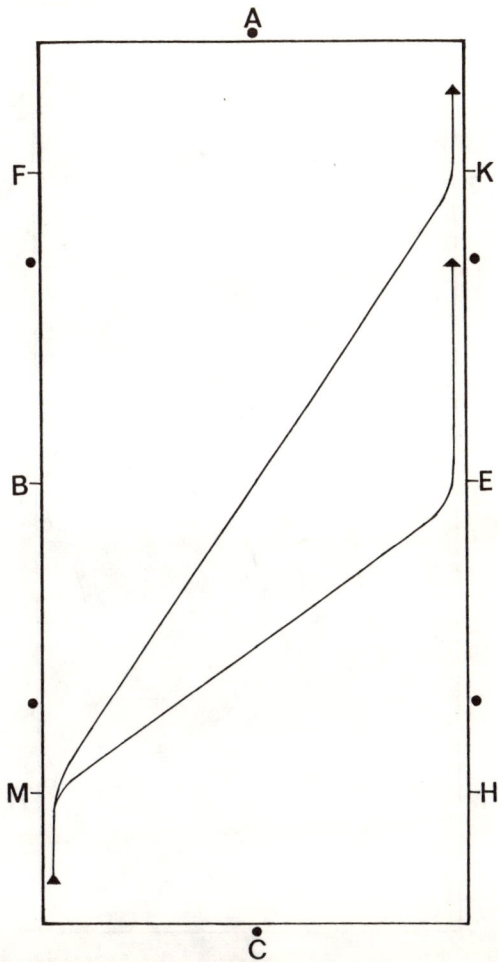

Figure 22: Diagonal Lines

Change rein through the diagonal (corner to corner = 45 meters)

> Walk = 25 seconds
> Trot = 15 seconds
> Canter = 10 seconds

Change through the short diagonal (corner to corner = 50 meters)

> Walk = 25 seconds
> Trot = 15 seconds
> Canter = 10 seconds

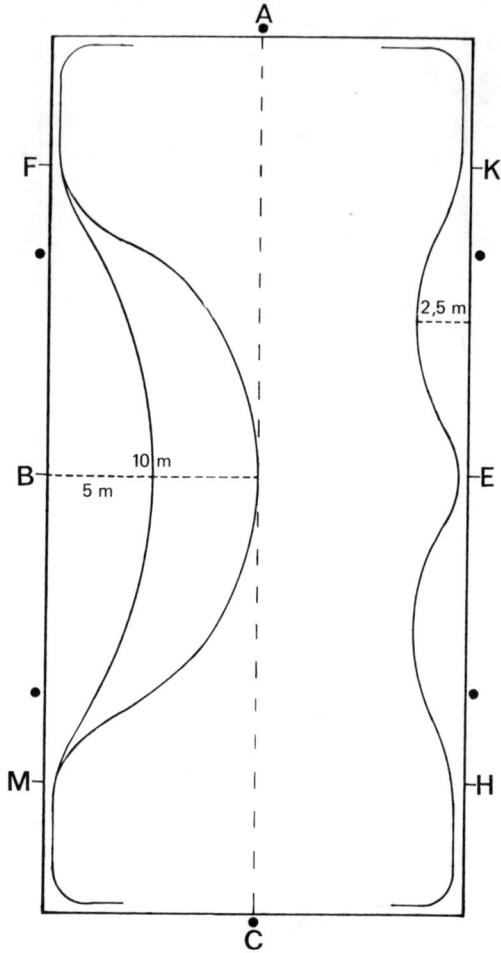

Figure 23: Serpentines along the long side, corner to corner

Single 5-meter serpentines = 42 meters
Walk = 20 seconds
Trot = 15 seconds
Canter = 10 seconds

Single 10-meter serpentines = 45 meters
Walk = 25 seconds
Trot = 15 seconds
Canter = 10 seconds

Double 2.5-meter serpentines = 42 meters
Walk = 20 seconds
Trot = 15 seconds
Canter = 10 seconds

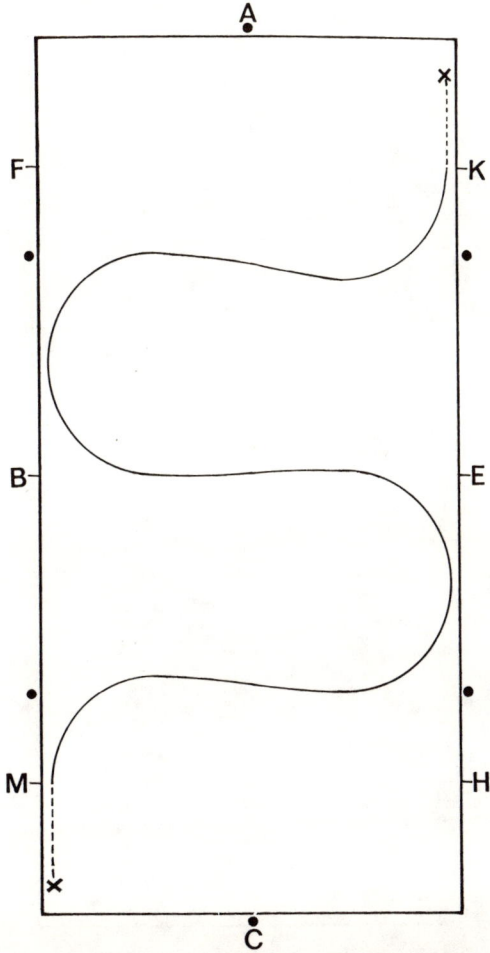

Figure 24: Four-loop serpentines, width of the arena (from corner to corner = 85 meters)

Walk = 45 seconds
Trot = 30 seconds
Canter (no change of lead) = 20 seconds
Canter (simple change of lead) = 25 seconds

Note: Serpentines are calculated from corner to corner, but, of course, are ridden from letter marker to letter marker.

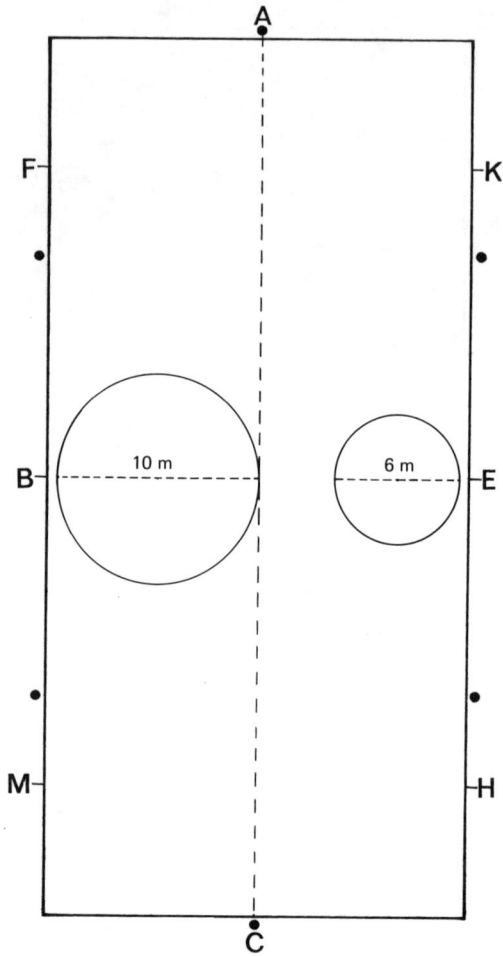

Figure 25: Voltés and Circles

10-meter circle = 30 meters

$$\begin{aligned} \text{Walk} &= 15 \text{ seconds} \\ \text{Trot} &= 10 \text{ seconds} \\ \text{Canter} &= 5 \text{ seconds} \end{aligned}$$

6-meter volté = 18 meters

$$\begin{aligned} \text{Walk} &= 10 \text{ seconds} \\ \text{Trot} &= 5 \text{ seconds} \\ \text{Canter} &= 5 \text{ seconds} \end{aligned}$$

FIGURES FOR THE EIGHT-HORSE QUADRILLE

Basic Rules

It is preferable to use simple figures ridden correctly. Use figures that are geometrically recognizable and strive towards symmetrical scenes that fill the arena. Begin the quadrille with easier figures, progressing towards the more complicated ones towards the end. Keep in mind that the proper distance between horses is a single horse's length. When riding single file, this might have to be shortened to allow all horses to fit along the long side.

Entrance, Starting Formations, Final Formations

• Enter at A to allow the file to enter on the center line. This can be done either single or double file. It could even be executed in fours.

• First formation and salute should be done at X or G. However, depending on where the audience is sitting, it might be done at D or along the short side at A.

Salute Formations

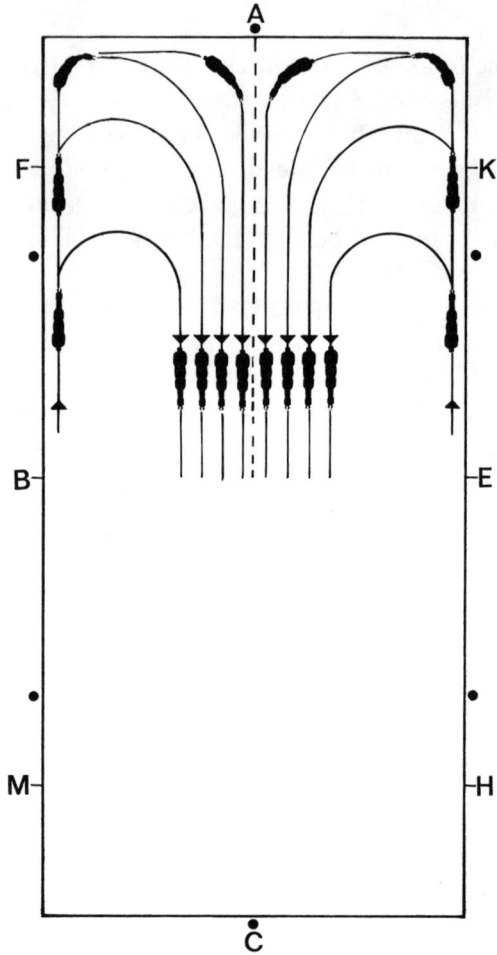

Figure 26: Front and Center

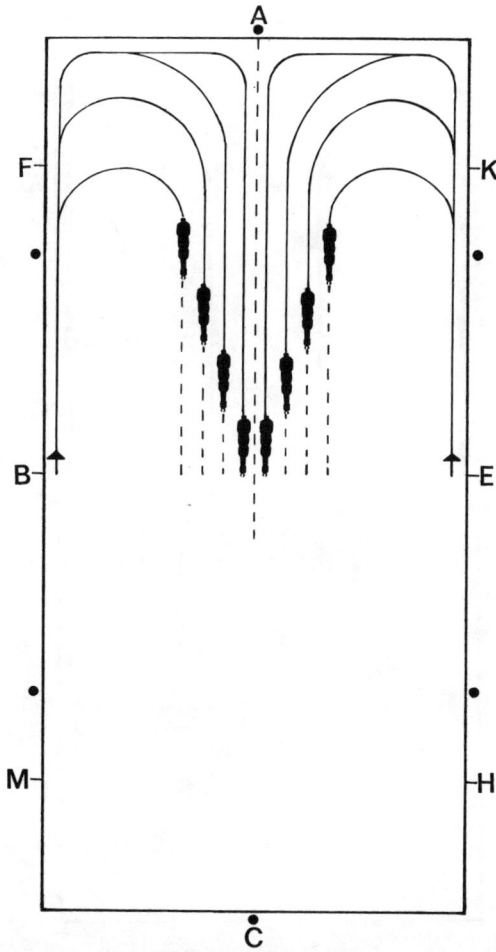

Figure 27: Echelon

There are two strides between horses. Horses' noses are at the level of the next horses' tails. This figure can also be ridden without the halt.

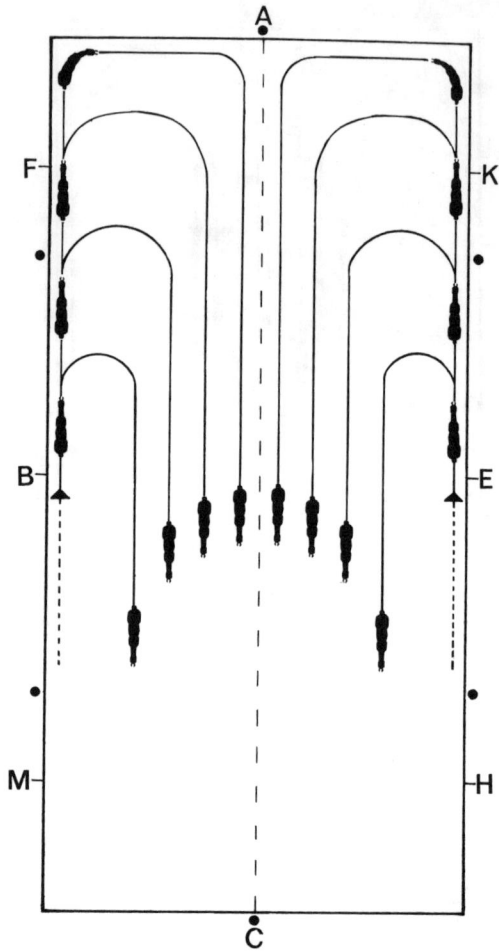

Figure 28: Half Circle

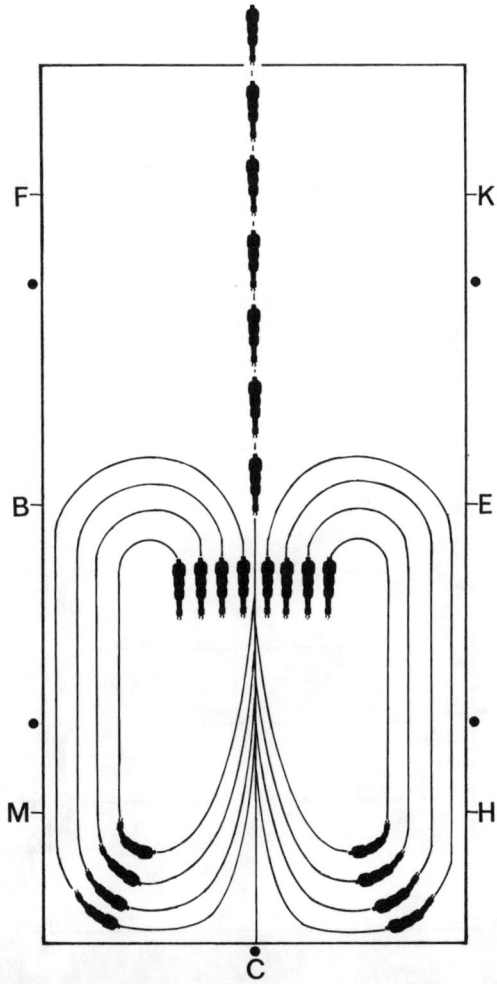

Figure 29: Single File on Center Line
Split at C into fours; half circle; front and center.

Single File, Eight-Horse Group

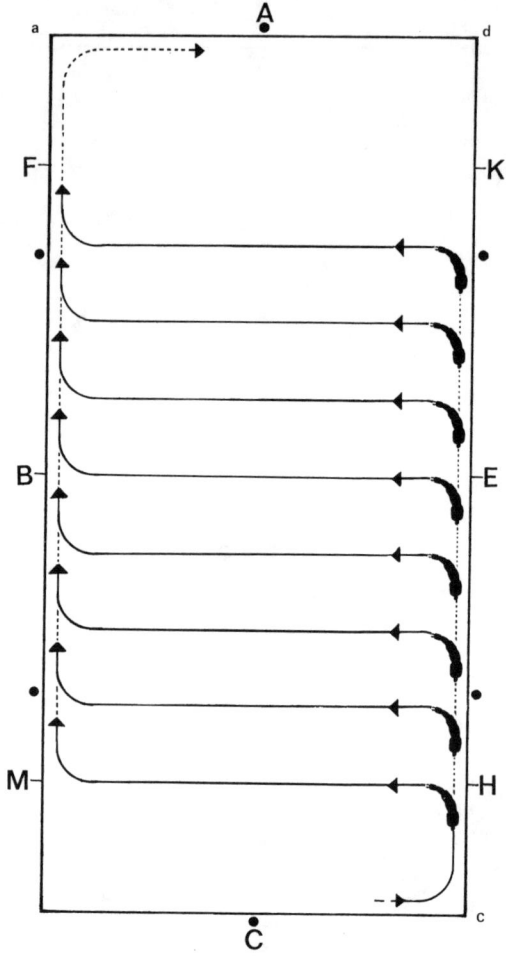

Figure 30: Single File, Eight Horses
Command: "File, turn left, march. From the long side, turn right, march."

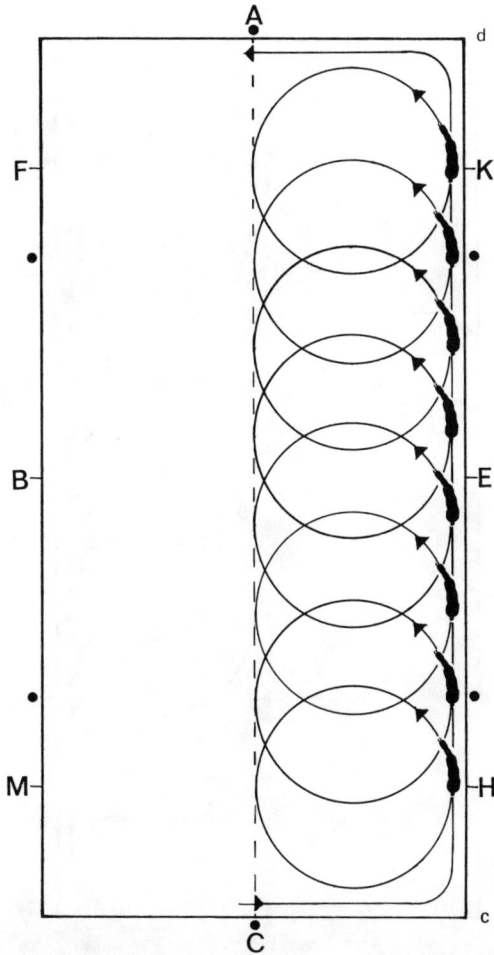

Figure 31: Volté on the Long Side
Command: "File, volté, march." Volté is ridden to the center line. Return to single file. This figure can also be ridden from the center line to the outside track.

c–d	40 meters
Volté	30 meters
c–d	70 meters

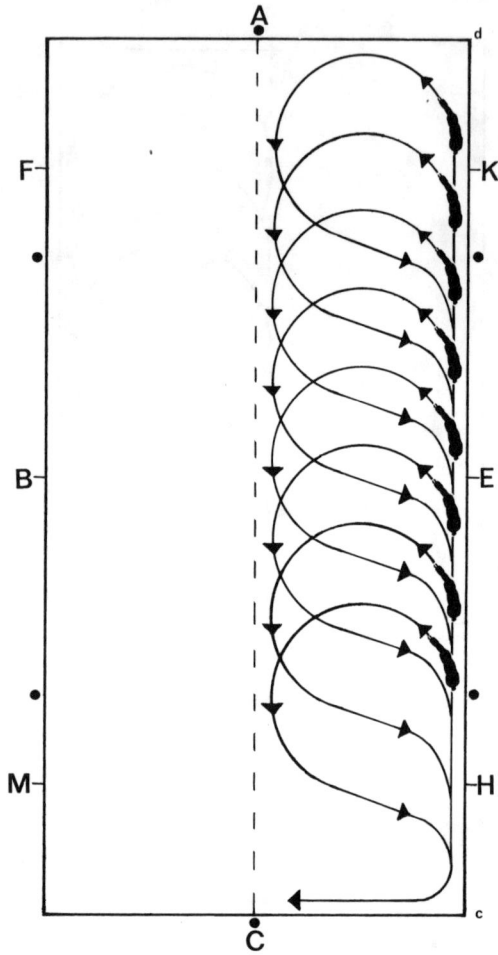

Figure 32: Half Circle and Reverse
Single file on the long side. Command: "File, reverse, march." The lead rider
should reverse in the corner.

c–d	40 meters
Half Circle	15 meters
d–c	40 meters
c–d–c	95 meters (distance for lead rider)

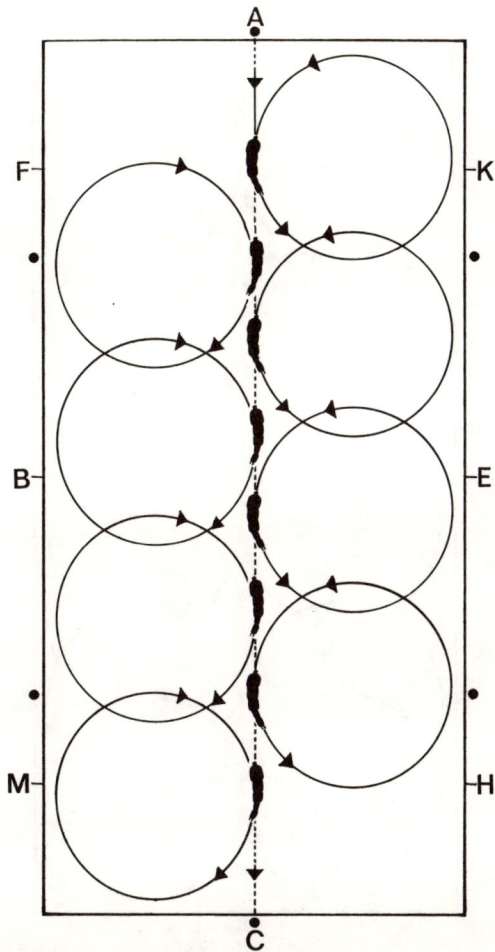

Figure 33: Circle Left and Right from Center Line
Single file on center line. Command: "Circle left and right, march." Riders 1, 3, 5, and 7 circle right; riders 2, 4, 6, and 8 circle left. Return to single file on the center line.

A–C	40 meters	
Circle	30 meters	
A–D	70 meters	

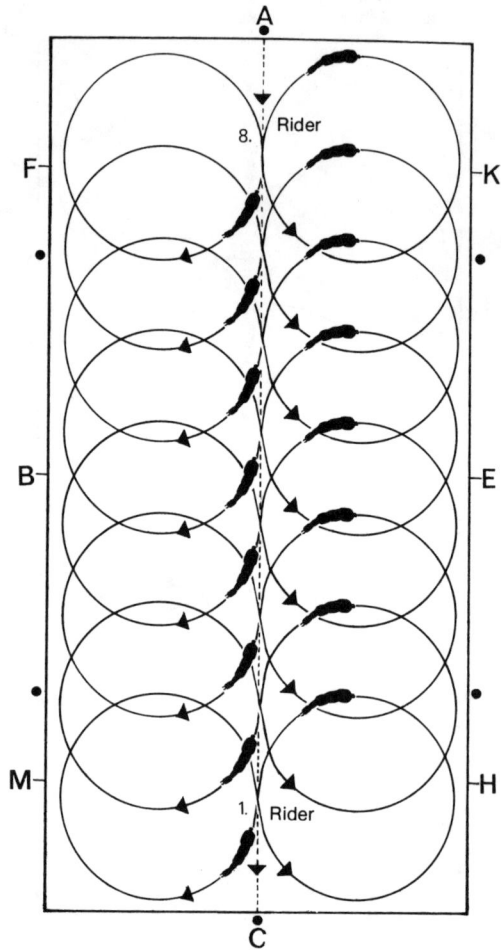

Figure 34: Figure-Eight

Single file down center line. Command: "File, figure-eight, march." All riders
volté right, return to center line, then volté left.

A–C	40 meters
Voltés	60 meters
A–C	100 meters

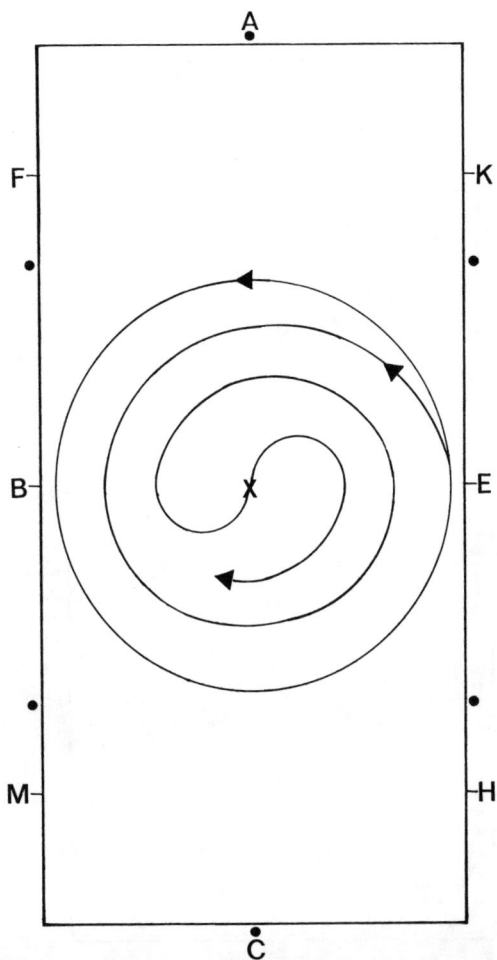

Figure 35: Middle Circle and Spiral-In
Middle circle left is followed by a spiral-in, then change of rein.

Circle (once around) 60 meters
Measure the spiral-in in seconds, not in meters.

Formal Pairs and Fours

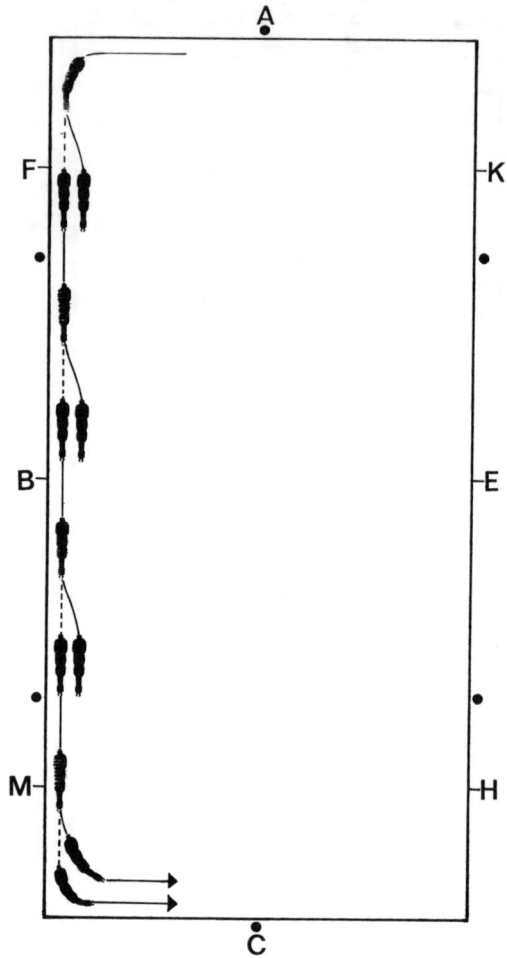

Figure 36: Form Pairs
Command: "Twos." Riders 1, 3, 5, and 7 shorten the stride; riders 2, 4, 6, and 8 lengthen the stride and move abreast of the first group. Lead slows the tempo.

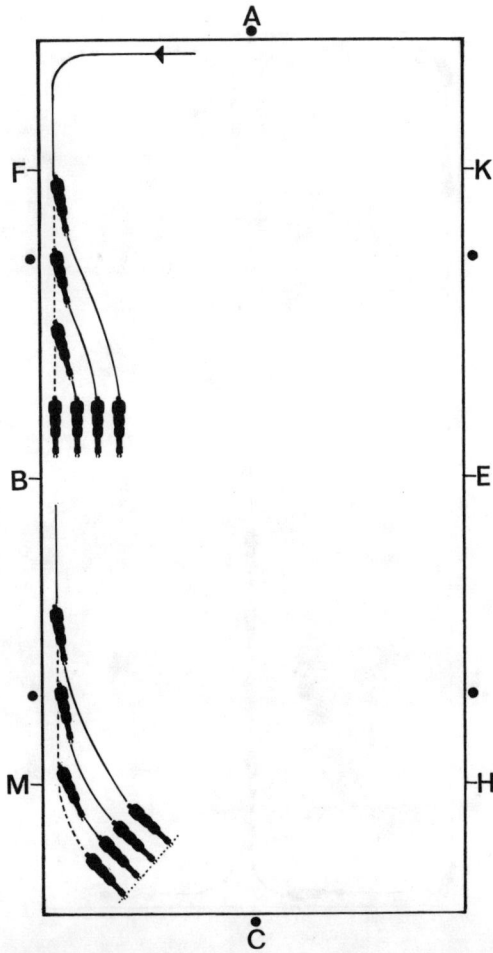

Figure 37: Form Fours
Command: "Fours." Riders 1 and 5 shorten the stride; all other increase the stride. This is best done going through a corner.

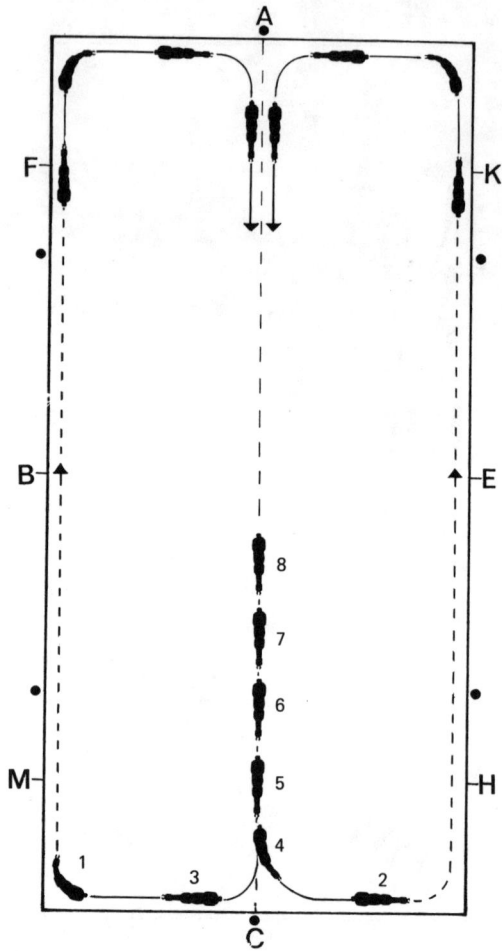

Figure 38: Forming Pairs Down Center Line
Single file down center line. Command: "Split right and left." Riders 1, 3, 5, and 7 go right; riders 2, 4, 6, and 8 go left. Then, "At A down center line in pairs."

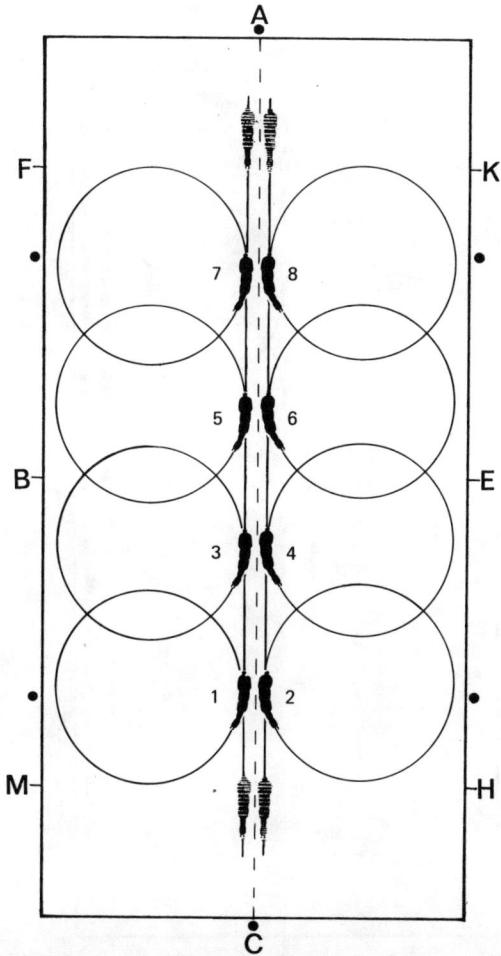

ure 39: Voltē Right and Left from Center Line
in pairs on center line. Command: "Voltē right and left, march." Pairs merge
on center line.

A–C	40 meters
Voltē	30 meters
A–C	70 meters

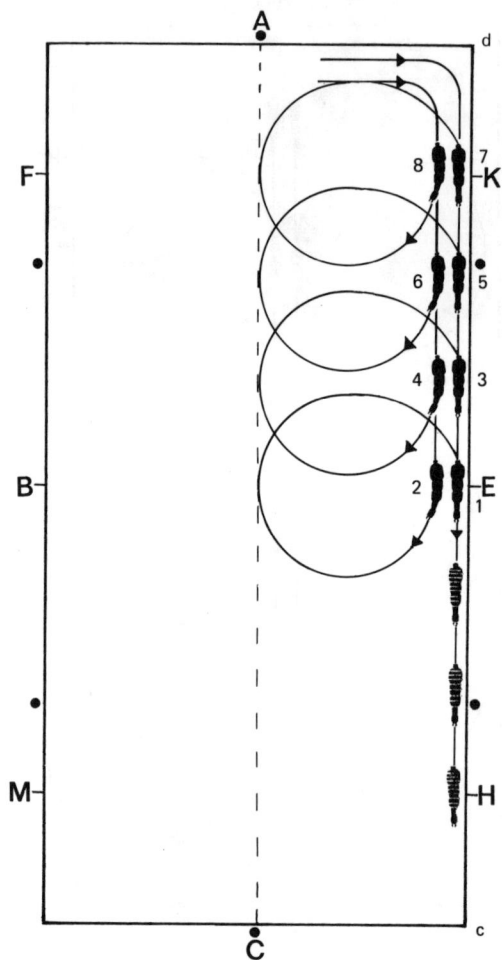

Figure 40: Inside Riders Volté
File in pairs along long side. First pair reaches E. Command: "Inside riders volté, march. Join end of file." When these riders have completed the volté, the lead rider (1) has reached H.

d–c	40 meters
Volté	30 meters
d–c	70 meters (inside riders)

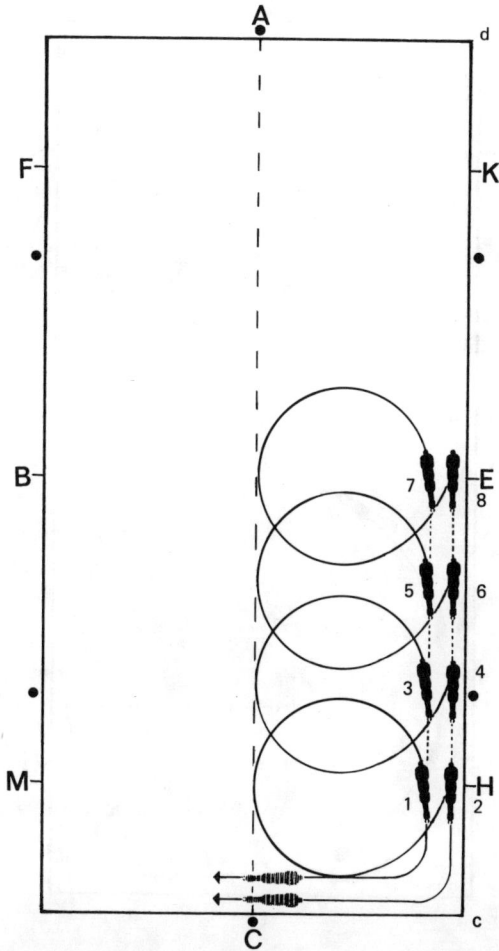

Figure 41: First Four Volté

The lead rider has reached H; all riders are in a single file on the long side, riders 1, 3, 5, and 7 ahead of 2, 4, 6, and 8. Command: "First four, volté, march. Form pairs." When these have completed their volté, rider 2 is at H.

d–c	40 meters
Volté	30 meters
d–c	70 meters (for first four riders)

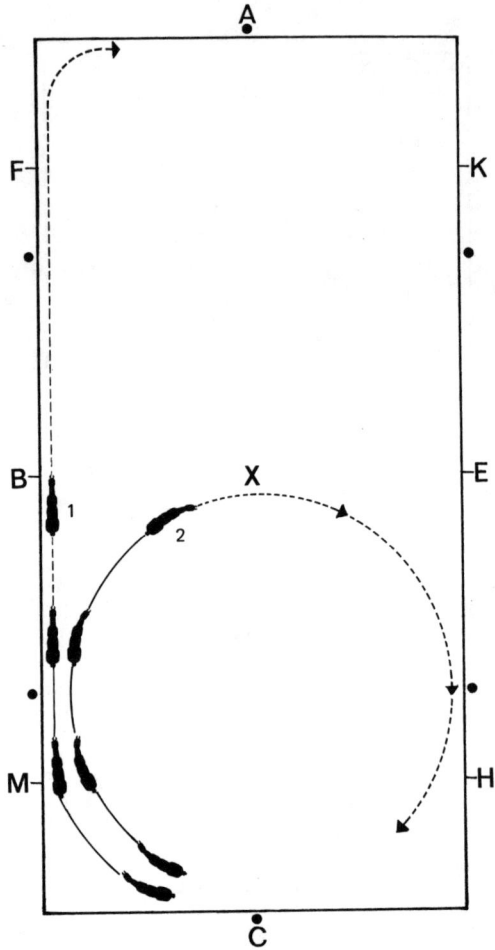

Figure 42: Inside Riders Circle
Pairs are on right rein. Command: "Inside riders circle; outside riders whole arena." Then, "Both groups whole arena." Now all riders are in single file on right rein.

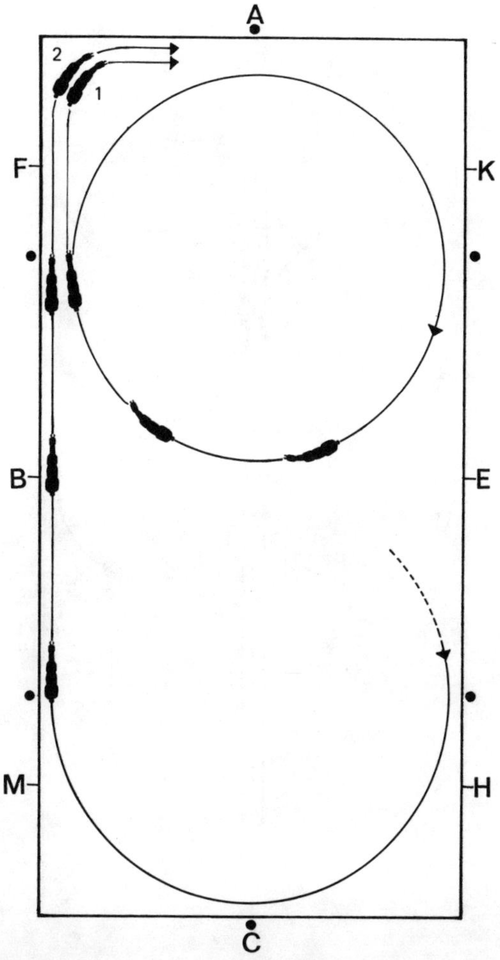

Figure 43: Reforming Pairs
Command: "First four circle, rest whole arena. Form pairs at F. Pairs, whole arena."

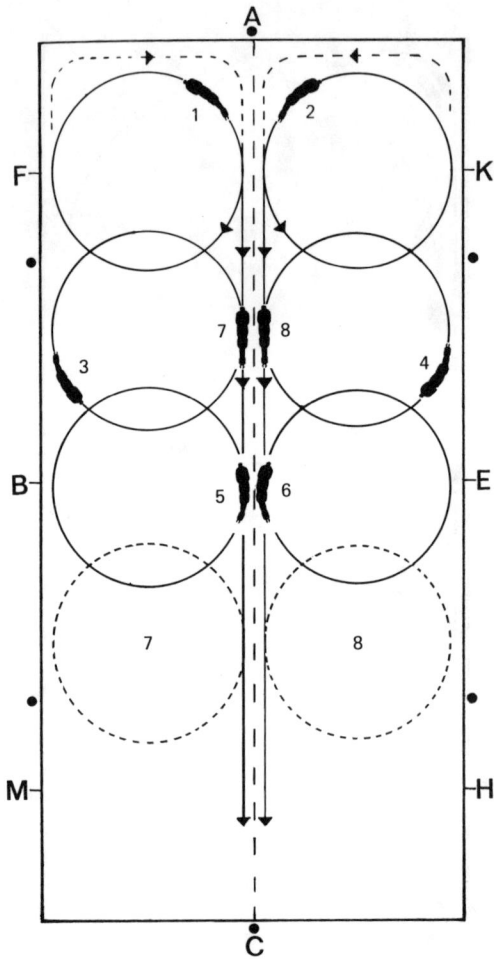

Figure 44: Consecutive Voltés
Without command, the first pair rides a volté across from F and K. The second pair continues down the middle line and rides their volté seven meters further down. The third pair rides the volté across from B and E. The fourth pair continues down the center line and rides the volté seven meters further down. Following the volté, the riders continue down center line in pairs.

A–C	40 meters
Volté	30 meters
A–C	70 meters

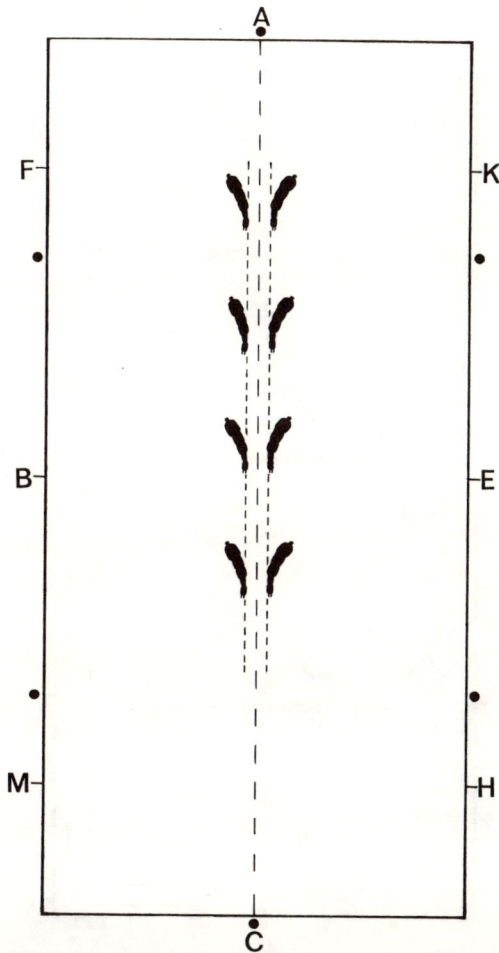

Figure 45: Snow Plow
Pairs down center line, swinging haunches out. At the lower levels this can be done as leg yielding; at the higher levels as travers.

A–C	40 meters
Extra Time	10 meters
A–C	50 meters

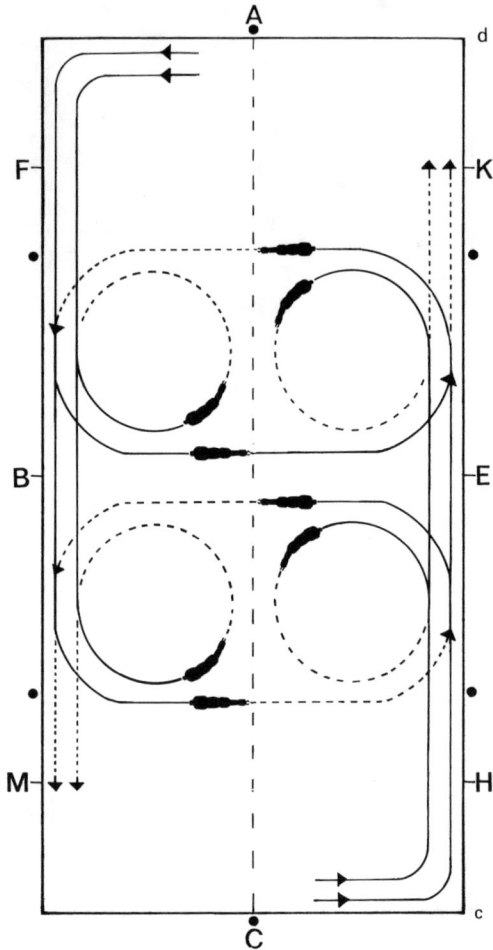

Figure 46: Echelon Volté

Two pairs are on each long side. Command: "Echelons, volté, march." All four pairs start the volté to the left. Inner riders ride the volté once around; outer riders ride only a quarter-volté, then cross to the opposite side forming a pair with the other inside rider. To return to the original formation, this is simply repeated.

c–d	40 meters
6-meter Volté	20 meters
c–d	60 meters

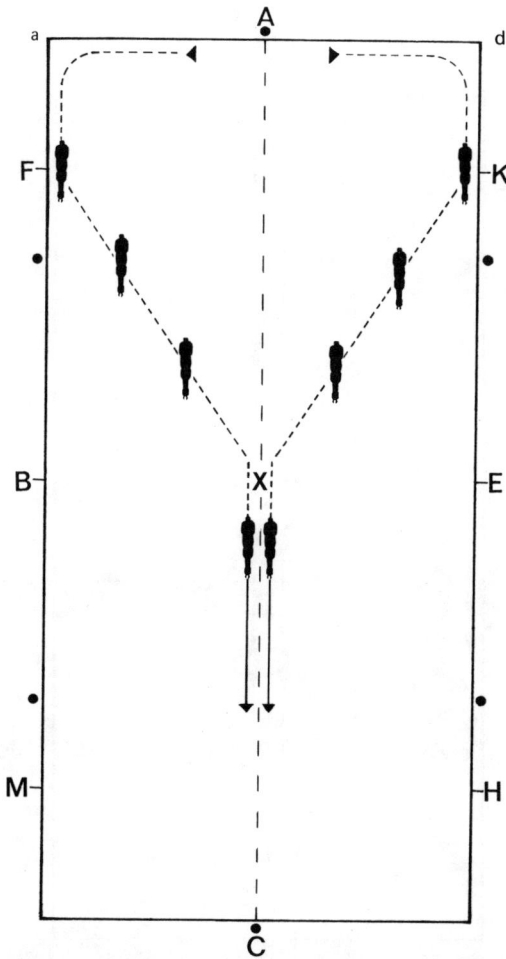

Figure 47: Leg Yield to X
Riders leg yield left and right to X where they form pairs and continue down
center line. At Training and First Levels, this should be done at the walk or collected trot; at higher levels it could be done as a half pass.

a–X	25 meters
X–C	20 meters
Extra Time	10 meters
a–C	55 meters

Opposing Pairs

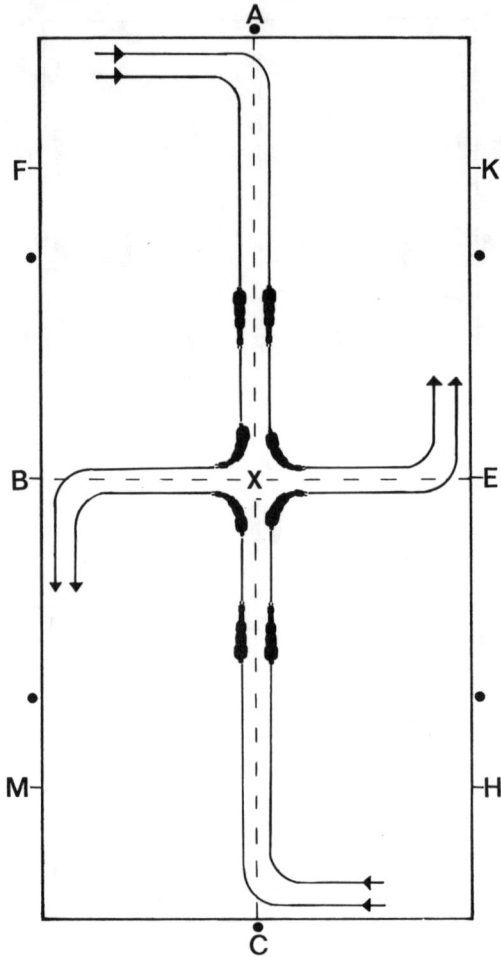

Figure 48: The Cross
Pairs ride toward one another along center line, splitting at X to form new pairs moving toward B and E, then changing rein. This can be repeated to restore the original order.

A–X–B–C 60 meters

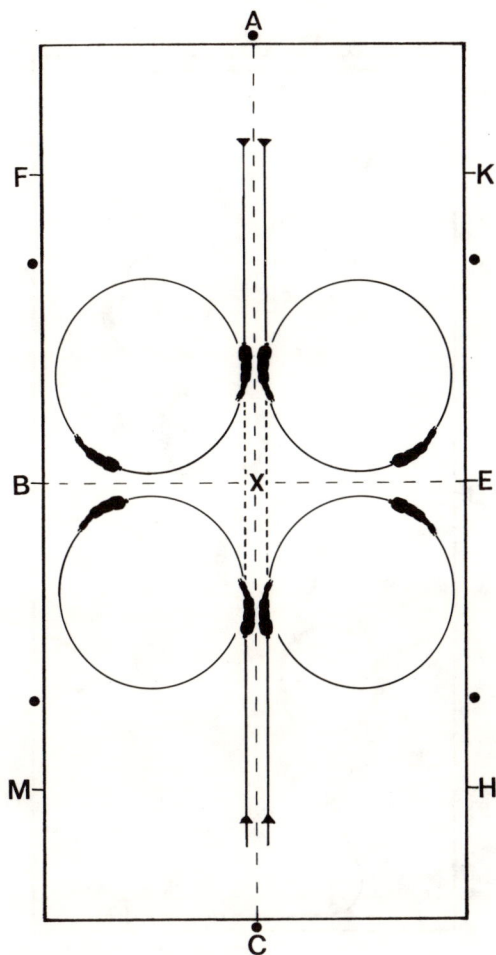

Figure 49: The Clover Leaf
Pairs ride toward one another along the center line. Three meters in front of X, they volté left and right, either once or twice around. They end the figure by returning to the center line and riding towards A and C whereby one pair opens to allow the second to pass through.

A–C	40 meters
Volté	30 meters
A–C	70 meters

Figures for Two Groups of Four Riders

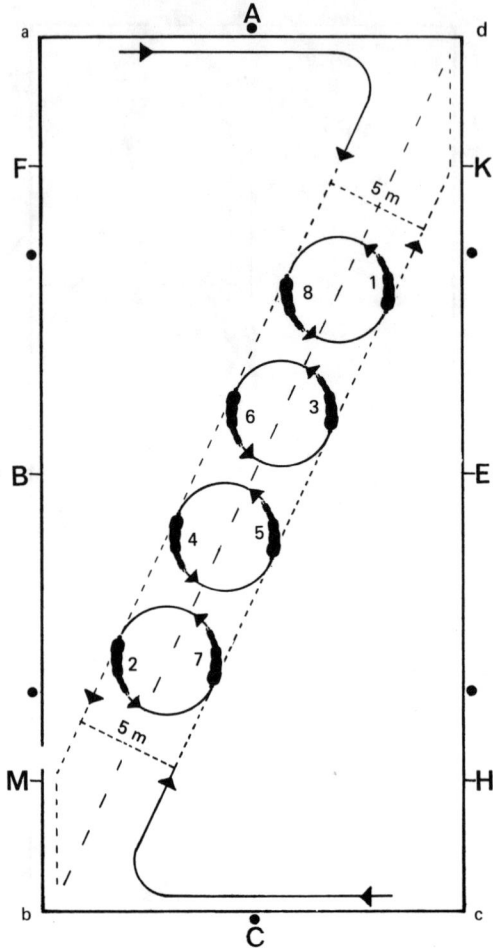

Figure 50: Carousel
Both groups are on right rein. Six meters before the corners b and d, both lead riders turn right, heading towards the diagonal markers. When all riders are on this line, they ride a 5-meter volté to the left around one another, continuing then in the original direction.

C–A	65 meters
5-Meter volté	15 meters
C–A	80 meters

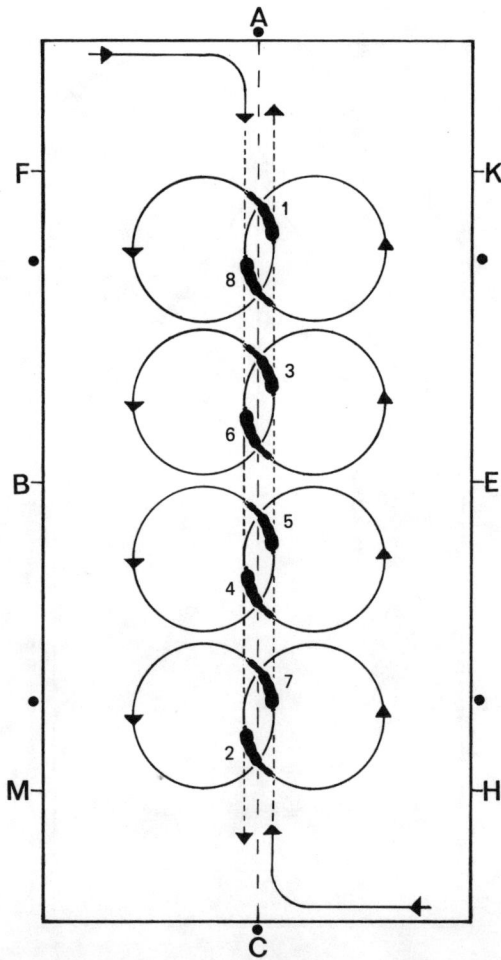

Figure 51: Tournez

Both groups are on opposite reins on the middle line. The command, "tournez," comes when the riders are directly across from their partners (1:8, 3:6, 5:4, 7:2). All turn at the same time in a volté left, once around.

C–A	40 meters
Volté	30 meters
C–A	70 meters

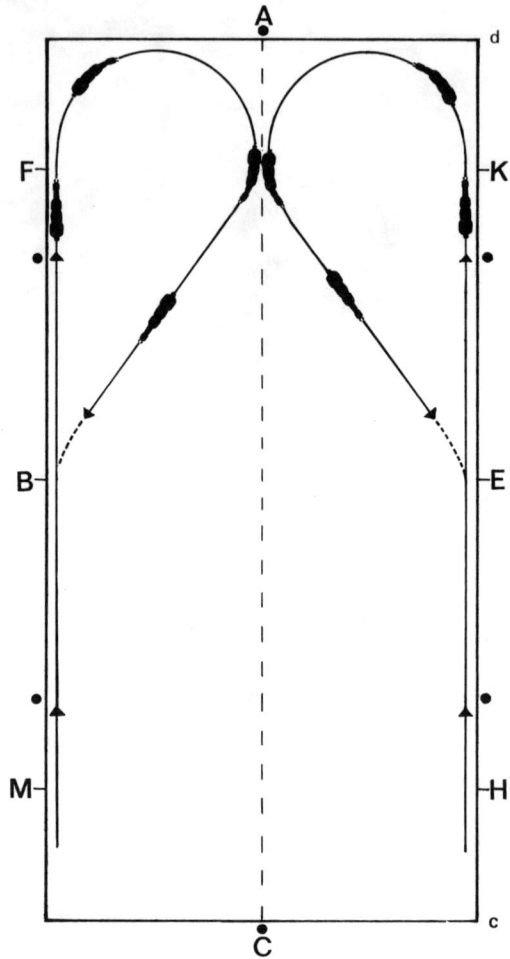

Figure 52: Half Turn and Reverse in the Corner
This is a simple but most effective figure.

c–d–c	80 meters
Half Volté	15 meters
c–d–c	95 meters

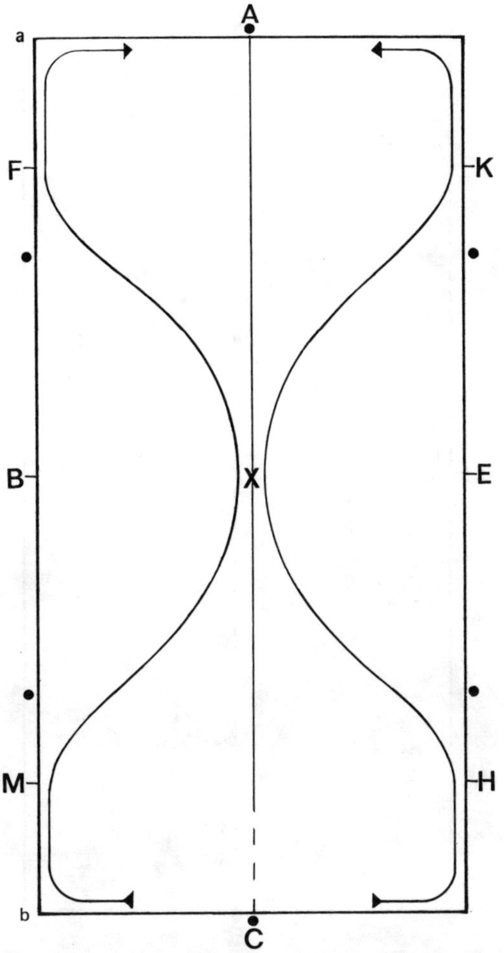

Figure 53: Simple Serpentine to X

a–b   45 meters

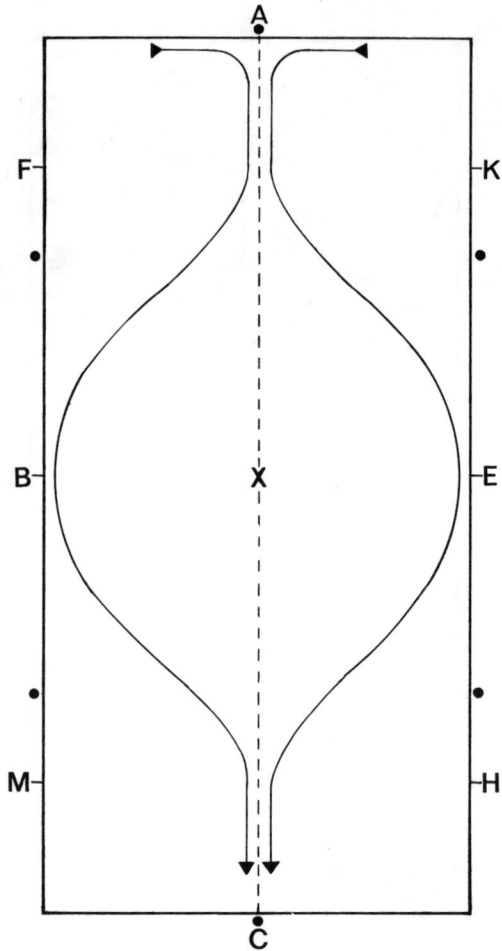

Figure 54: Simple Serpentine Along the Center Line to B and E Pairs on the center line. Begin serpentine across from F and K.

A–C   45 meters

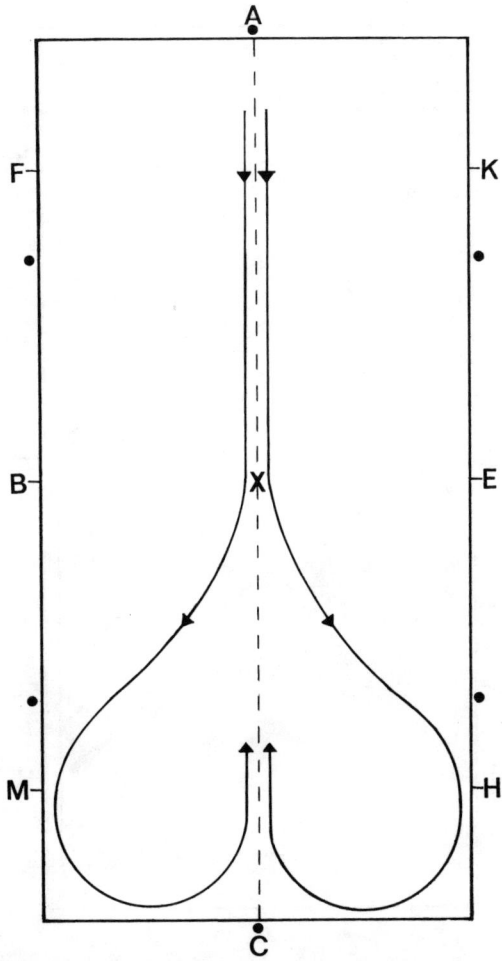

Figure 55: The Heart
Pairs on center line. At X, ride a softly curved line to M and H, returning at C to the center line.

A–C 50 meters

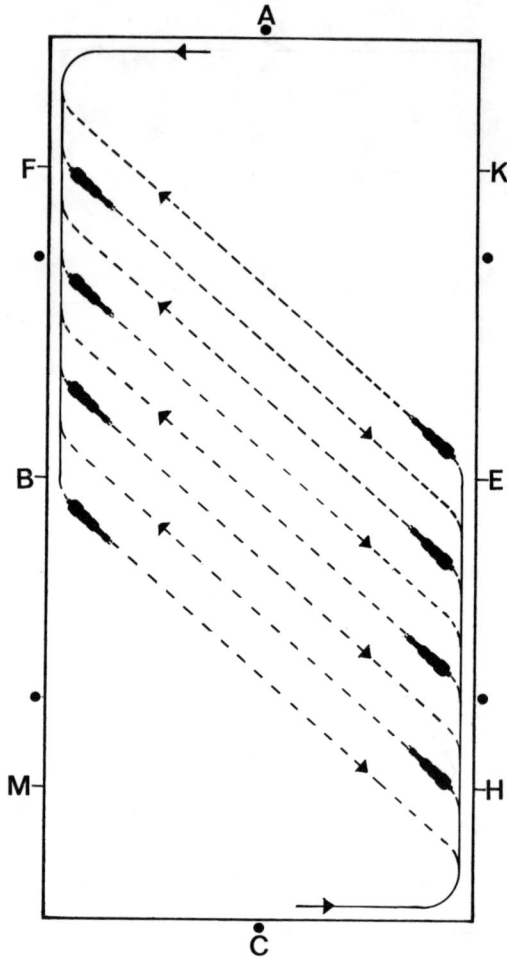

Figure 56: Short Diagonal Left
Both groups on left rein without spaces. At E and B, command, "Short diagonals left." Both leaders ride a straight line towards a point approximately 3 meters before the corners.

C–A   70 meters

Figures on the Circle

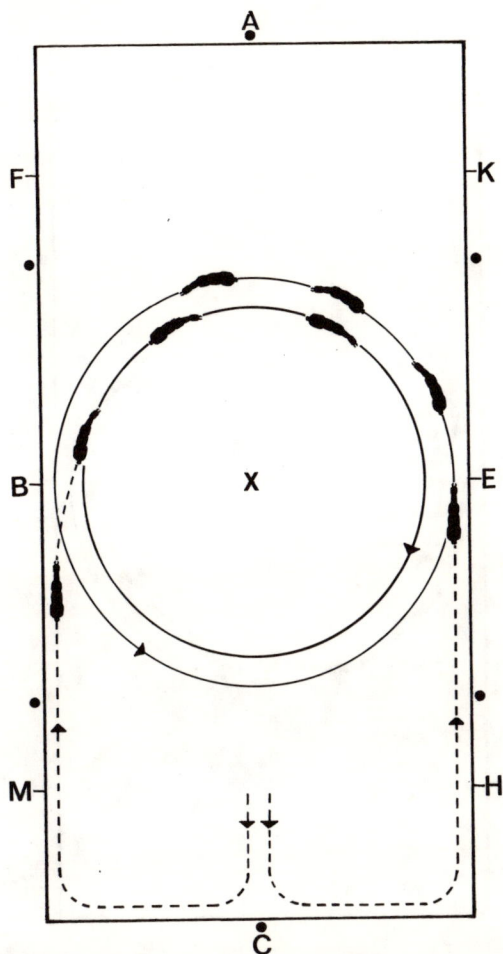

Figure 57: Opposing Groups on the Middle Circle
Two groups ride the middle circle on opposite reins beginning the circle at B and E.

Outer Circle   60 meters

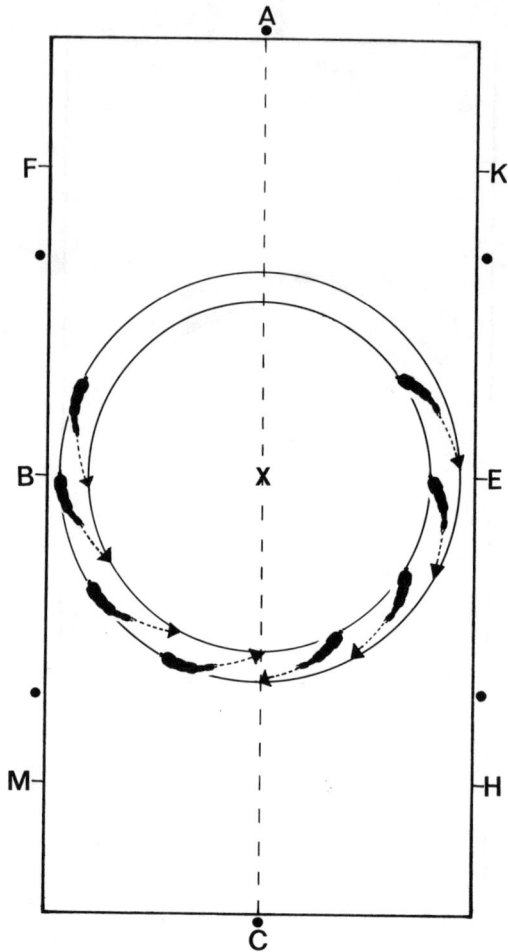

Figure 58: Changing on the Middle Circle
As in Figure 57. The lead riders must meet on the center line. The outer circle increases the tempo, the inside circle decreases the tempo. At a designated point on the circle line, the lead riders change circles followed by all other riders.

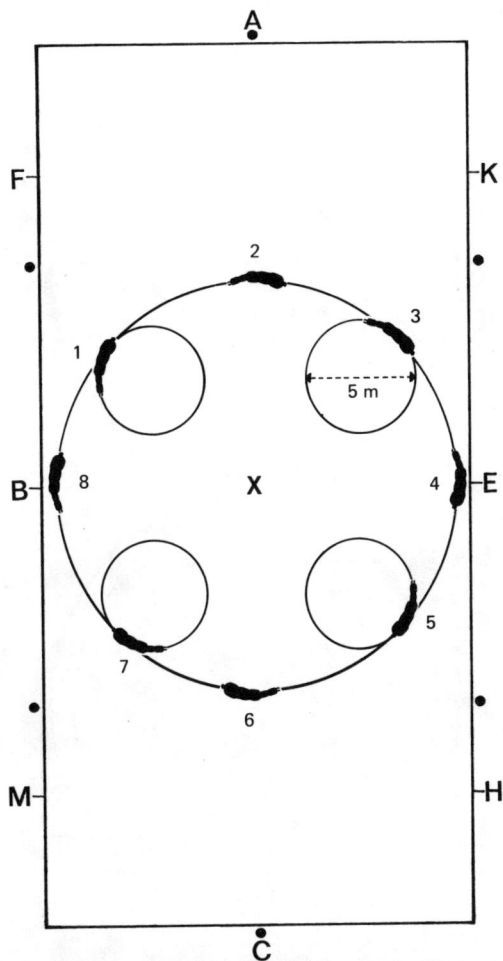

Figure 59: Volté on the Middle Circle
The riders are single file on the middle circle. Riders 1, 3, 5, and 7 simultaneous-ly execute a 5-meter volté. Riders 2, 4, 6, and 8 have proceeded approximately 15 meters further along the circle line. They now ride a 5-meter volté to restore the original order.

Circle (once around)	60 meters
5-Meter Volté	15 meters
	75 meters

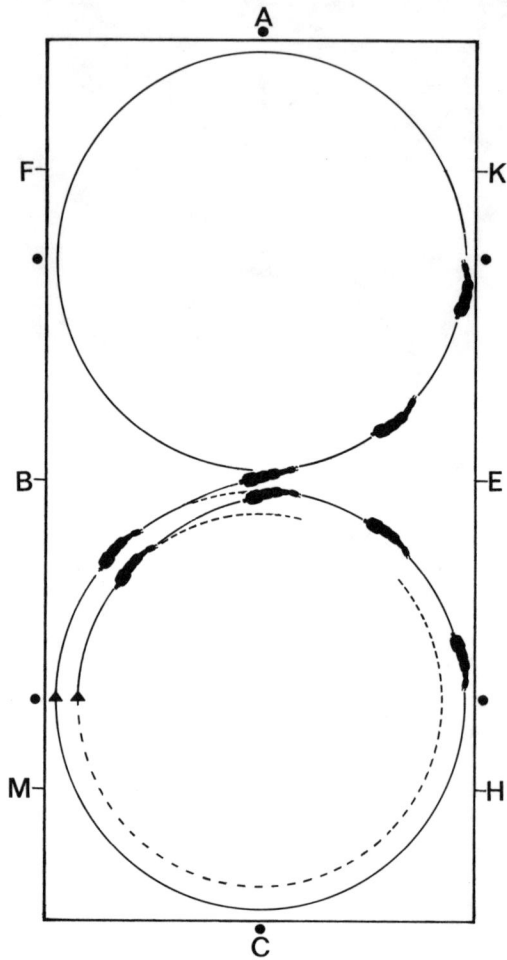

Figure 60: Outer Riders Change Rein from Circle to Circle
Pairs are on lower circle, right rein. Command: "Outside riders change rein to the upper circle." Lead riders should then keep eye contact and meet at X. The groups stay on the two circles.

Circle (once around)   60 meters

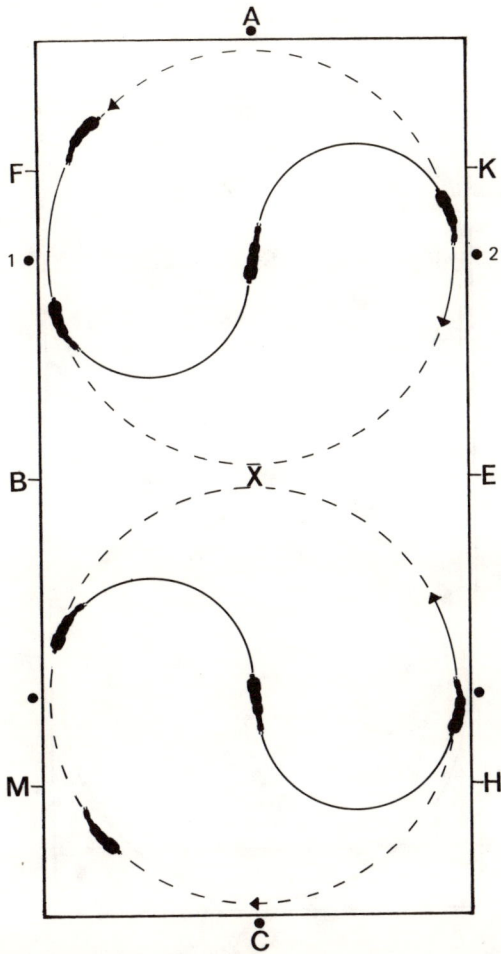

Figure 61: Change Through the Circles
Command: "Both groups change through the circles." The two groups then form pairs again at X and continue on a single circle either to the left or the right.

Circle Point 1 to Circle Point 2   30 meters

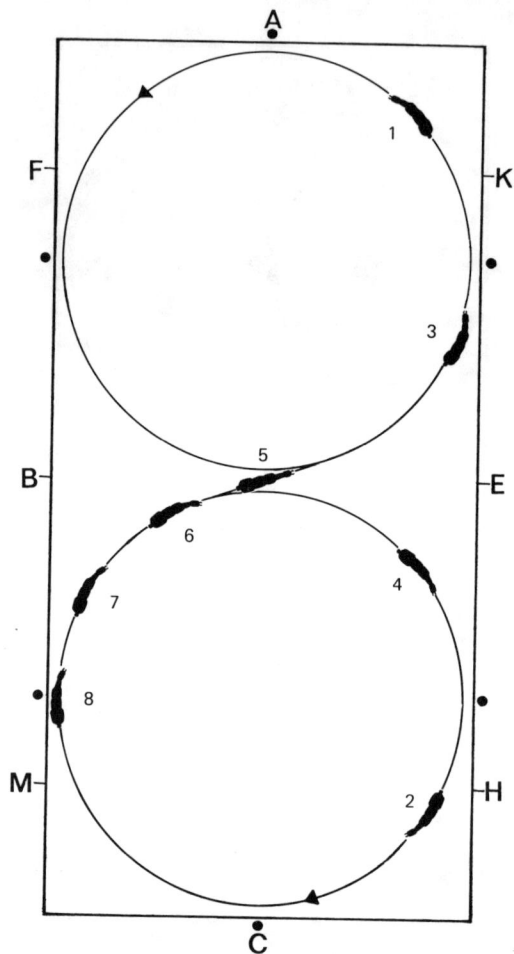

Figure 62: At X Divide and Change
Single file on lower circle at C. Command: "Alternate riders change rein to upper circle." Maintain tempo and spacing.

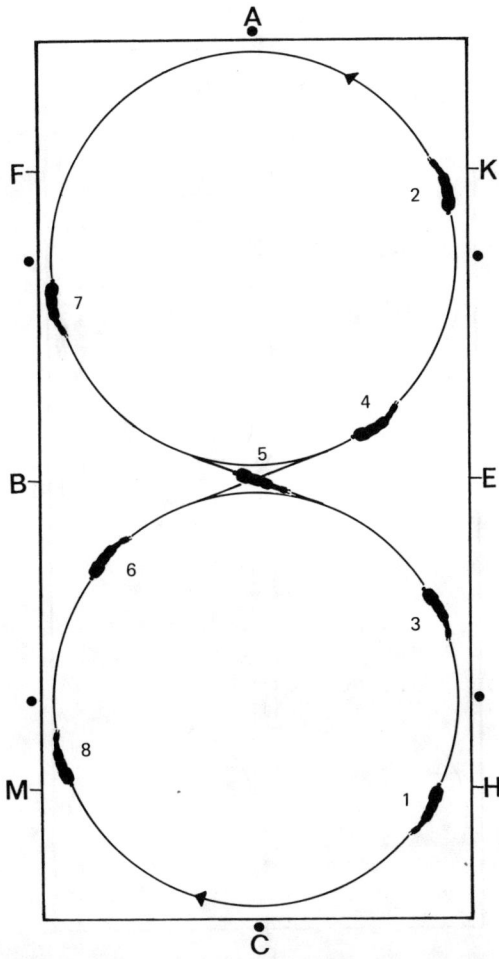

Figure 63: Change Rein to Opposite Circle
Command: "Both groups change rein to opposite circle." In making the change, the groups cross through X.

Voltés in the Corner

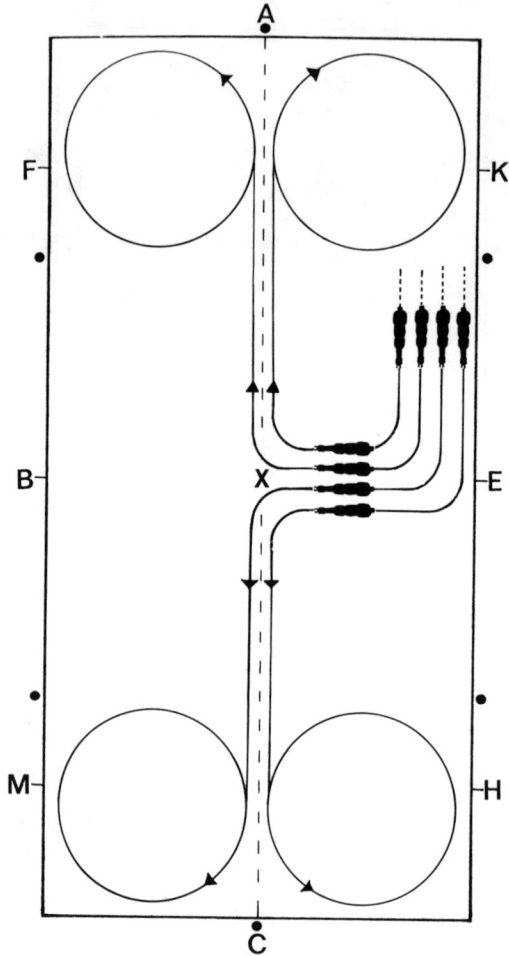

Figure 64: Volté in the Corners
Fours formation moves to volté in corners. Split into pairs at X, riding towards A and C. At A and C, pairs split and volté in the corners, twice around.

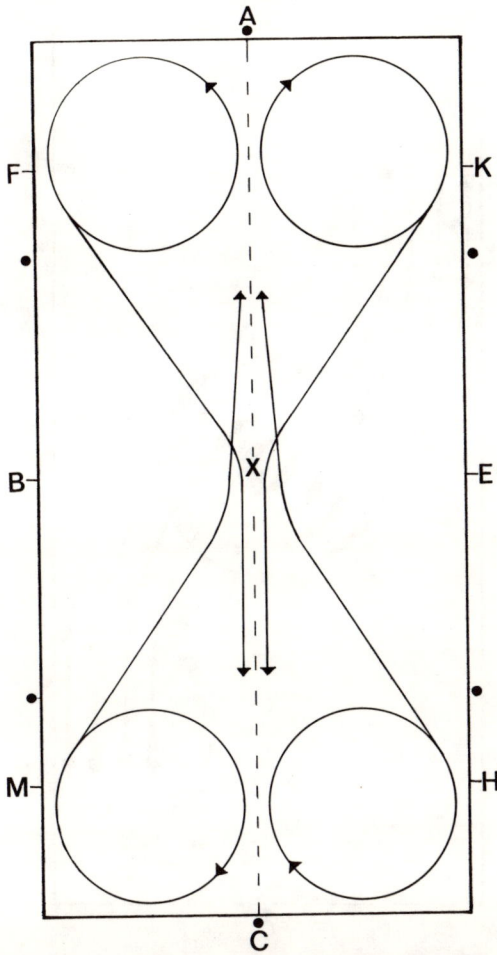

Figure 65: Ending the Corner Volté Formation
Riders move out of the volté simultaneously and head toward X. The pair coming from A merges closely; the pair coming from C widens to let the other pair pass.

Formation and Ending from X to X; Volté two times around:

X–A	20 meters
2½ Voltés	75 meters
F/K–X	15 meters
	110 meters

The Windmill

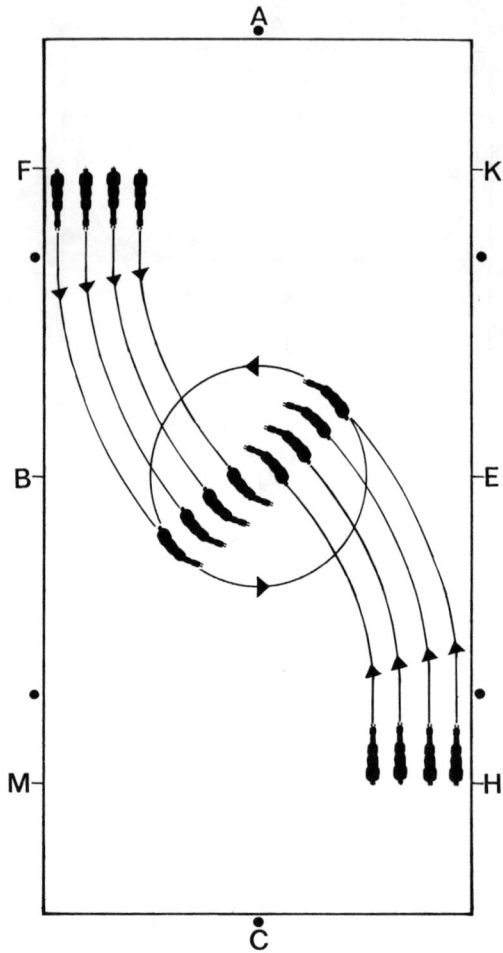

Figure 66: Forming the Windmill
A really well-done windmill is the highpoint of every quadrille, both for the audience and the riders. It should be performed close to the end of the quadrille.

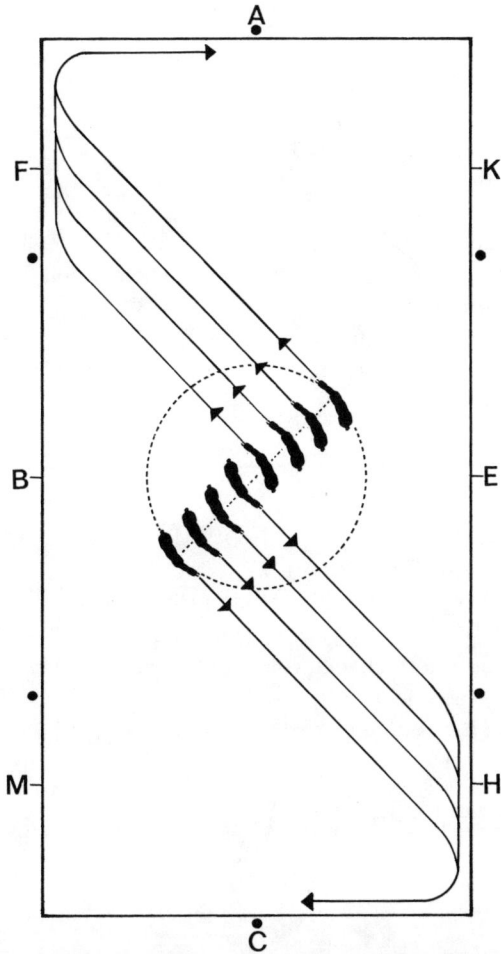

Figure 67: Ending the Windmill
There are quite a few possibilities here. The riders could leave the formation in
blocks of four, in pairs, or singly.

SAMPLE QUADRILLE
FOR TRAINING OR FIRST LEVEL

Formation Facing Front: Salute

		Meters	Time
Walk	Proceed at walk from middle of formation toward C		
C	Split right and left		
M & H	Change through diagonal		
A	Down center line in pairs. Volté right and left on command.		
C	Split right and left		
M & H	Simple serpentine to X		
	Total work at the walk:	220 m = 1.50	

Trot			
H–A	Trot (with music)		
A	Echelon to C (see figure 27)		
C	Pairs left rein, 20-meter circle (1½ times around)		
X	Outside riders change rein to upper circle (1½ times) (see figure 60)		
F & M	Both groups change through the circles (see figure 61)		
	Total work at the trot:	260 m = 1.20	

Canter			
X	Working canter (with music) on two circles (twice around)		
	Total work at the canter:	120 m = 0.30	

Trot			
X	Form pairs, left rein, whole arena (once around).		
C	In pairs on center line		
X	Half turn and reverse, splitting left and right		
C	Split left and right		
A	In single file on center line		
X	Turn right		

B	Middle circle, right, once around then spiral in and out (see figure 35)
E	Go large, single file, right rein
H–C	Form pairs (see figure 36)
M	Inside riders 20-meter circle, outside riders go large. After one circle, inside riders also go large.
E & B	Groups turn right, passing left shoulder to left shoulder. Both groups, left rein.
C–H & F–A	Form pairs (see figure 36)
K–A & M–C	Form fours
F & H	Fours change rein through the diagonal
X	Windmill, left, once around (see figures 66–67)
H & F	Fours go large, once around
H & F	Single file
M & K	Change through the diagonal
	Total work at the trot: 1,100 m = 5.30

Canter

A & C	Canter. First group circle; second group whole arena.
K	Form pairs, 20-meter circle, once around
A	Whole arena in pairs, once around
	Total work at the canter: 240 m = 0.50

Trot

A	Trot and down center line in pairs
C	Split left and right, whole arena
A	Down center line. When music ends, halt and salute.
I	Final formation, "Front"
	Total work at the trot: 130 m = 0.40

Total Time	10.40

SAMPLE SECOND LEVEL
QUADRILLE FOR FOUR HORSES

Walk

A	Enter single file on center line. Salute at the walk.
C	Split, change rein through diagonal to X
X	Form pairs, down center line
A	Split
F & K	Leg yield to X, form pairs, down center line

Total work at the walk: 170 m = 1.25

Trot

C	Split, change rein through diagonal
A	In pairs, down center line; first pair, volté left and right
X	Second pair, volté left and right
C	Split, change through the diagonal to X
X	In pairs down center line
A	In fours, right rein
E	Fours, turn right
B	In pairs, turn right and left
A & C	In pairs, down center line
X	"Clover Leaf," twice around (see figure 49)
X	In pairs down center line. Riders 1 and 3 move together; riders 2 and 4 open.
A & C	In pairs, right rein
M & K	Change through the diagonal whereby one pair opens to let the second ride through.
C & A	Pair at C circles; pair at A whole arena
M	Form fours
H	Inside pair 20-meter circle, then whole arena
E & B	Echelon volté, twice around (see figure 46). In the following corner, single file.
F & H	Change through the diagonal, forming "Carousel" to the left (see figure 50).
A & C	Single file on center line, passing left to left
C & A	Everyone left rein. Riders 1 and 2 whole arena; 3 and 4, 20-meter circle
M	3 and 4 close behind 1 and 2, single file
A	20-meter circle, single file. Walk.

Total work at the trot: 1035 m = 5.20

Canter

A	Pick up canter (with music) on circle, left rein, single file
A	Single file down center line
C	Single file, circle left, 1½ times around
X	Riders 2 and 4 change to upper circle, no change of leads, as riders 1 and 3 continue on lower circle. Once around (see figure 60).
X	Riders 2 and 4 change back to circle at C. Single file, 1½ times around.
C	Single file, whole arena
K	Single file, half turn and reverse in corner (see figure 52)
B	Change leads through the trot. (Everyone changes when lead rider reaches B.)
F	Simultaneous volté when lead rider reaches F. Command: "March!"
A	Group turns right when centered at A. In fours down center line.
G	Simple change of rein. Split, one pair left, the other right. In the next corners, single file.
E & B	Consecutive voltes (see figure 44)
F & K	Single file, half turn and reverse, no change of lead (see figure 52).
M & H	Change rein through diagonal; no change of lead
K & F	Form pairs
A	In fours down center line
C	Split into pairs
A	In fours down center line. Final formation.
X	Salute

Total work at the canter: 805 m = 2.45

Total Time 9.10

In these examples, I have left off suggestions for collection and extentions of gait as these should evolve from the music.

Of course, it is always possible to choose the music first and then build in the figures as I've described in previous chapters. See "The Quadrille with Continuous Music" in Chapter 5 and Chapter 6, "From Theory to Practice."

Appendix

RECORDINGS

Listed below are the works mentioned in *Riding to Music* which are currently available in the United States. Where possible those recordings are listed which contain several pieces suitable to ride to.

Adam	*Giselle*	*Art of the Prima Ballerina* Decca SET 254215
Alford	*Colonel Bogey March*	*Marching Along* Mercury SRI/MRI 75004
Auber	Overtures	Fonit/Cetra LMA 3013
		Pops Round the World Phillips Dig 400 071-2
Bach, J.C.	Symphonia in B-flat Major	Phillips 6768 336
Bach, J.S.	Brandenburg Concerti	Deutsche Grammaphone DG Arc. Dig 410 500/1-2
Beethoven	*York March*	*Radetzky March* DG Priv 2535/3335 647
	Overtures	Berlin Philharmonic/Karajan DG Priv 2726/079
Berlioz	*La Damnation de Faust*	Phillips Dig 6769/7654089
Bizet	*L'Arlésienne* and *Carmen*	CBS 60142 40 with Stokowski
Borodin	*Polovetzian Dances*	Decca SPA 281
Brahms	*Hungarian Dances*	Decca Jub 411 725-1/4

Cherubini	*Anacréon*	*Opera Overtures & Intermezzi* HMV Dig ASD/Tcc-ASD 4072
Delibes	*Sylvia*	London JL/5-41071
Donizetti	*La Favorite*	Phillips 9500 673/7300 768
Enesco	*Rumanian Rhapsody*	Mercury SRI/MRI 75018 London Symphony with Dorati
Glinka	*Ruslan and Ludmilla*	*Favorites of the Philharmonic* MFP-MFP TC MFP 1001 London Philharmonic Orchestra
	A Life for the Czar	HMV SLS 165 112-3
Gounod	*Faust*	Phillips Dig 6514/7337 070 Rotterdam Philharmonic
Handel	*Music for the Royal Fireworks*	DG 413 148-4 Berlin Philharmonic/Kubelik
	Concerti grossi	DG Arc Dig 410 8991-4
Haydn, Franz Joseph	Symphonies no. 93, 94, 101, and 104	Deutsche Grammaphone
	Symphony no. 88	CRD CRD 1070/CRD 4070
Haydn, Michael	*Turkish March*	*Festival of Marches* Phillips Dig 6725/7655010
Herold	*Zampa*	*Famous Overtures* Decca 410 294-4
Heuberger	*An Opera Ball*	*Overtures of Old Vienna* Decca Jub. JB47
Khachaturian	*Gayane*	Decca SXL/KSXC 6000 Vienna Philharmonic
Kopetzsky	*Egerland March*	*Radetzky March* DG Priv 2535/3335 647
Kreisler	*Caprice viennois*	HMV ASD 3258 I. Perlman
Lanner	Waltzes	Phillips Dig 6514/7337 Vienna Volk Opera Orchestra
Leonhard	*Prince Eugen*	*Radetzky March* DG Priv 2535/3335 647
Liszt	*Les Préludes*	Decca VIV/KVIC 37 Vienna Philharmonic
	Hungarian Rhapsodies	Mercury SRI/MRI 75018
Lortzing	*Casanova* *Undine* *Zar und Zimmermann*	ZMI IC 183 29302

Massenet	*The Cid*	HMV Green ESD/TC ESD 7040
Montiverdi	*L'Orfeo*	DG Arc 2723 018 (3) (complete)
Mozart	Symphonies	Deutsche Grammaphone
	March in D Major	Saga 5478
	Horn Concerto in D Major	Tel AW6,41272/CX4 41277
	Overtures	HMV Dig CDC 747014-2
	A Little Night Music	
	Serenata notturna	CRD 1040/CRDC 4040
	Idomeneo	DG 2740 19/3371 043
	Haffner Serenade	Phillips 6770 043
Offenbach	Overtures	Phillips Dig 6514/7337
Parlow	*Amboss Polka*	*Riding Marches* Ariola-Eurodisk 218 & 271
Ponchielli	*Dance of the Hours (La Gioconda)*	
	Cinderella	HMV Green ESD/TC ESD 7115
Ravel	*Bolero*	Decca Jub JB/KJBC 133
Rimsky-Korsakov	*Russian Easter Overture*	*A Russian Festival Gala* CCP CFP/TC CFP 4397
Rossini	Overtures	CFP CFP/TC 40379 Philadelphia Philharmonic
	Journey to Reims	Decca Dig 400 049-2
Schrammel	*Vienna Forever*	*Radetzky March* DG Priv 2535/3335 647
Schubert	*Overture in the Italian Style*	
	Symphony no. 6 in C Major	Decca Jub JB/KJBC 76
	Rosamunde	
	Five German Dances	Phillips Seq 6527/7311 056
Smetana	*The Two Widows*	Sup 1122 041/1 Prague National Theater Orchestra
Spohr	*Salute to Kiel*	*Riding Marches* Ariola-Eurodisk 218 & 271
Strauss, Johann, Sr.	Marches	*A Strauss Gala* Decca D145 D 4/k145 K44 set w/ W. Boskovsky

Strauss, Johann, Jr.	Marches	Decca D145 PRTGSGC 1266 2008
	Polkas	Decca 411932-2
	Waltzes	*The World of Strauss* Decca SPA KCSP 312
Strauss, Josef	*Fire Festival*	Decca 411932-2
Strauss, Richard	*Also sprach Zarathustra*	DG 2530 402/330 375 Berlin Philharmonic
Suppé	Overtures	Decca Jub JB/KJBC 133 DG Priv 2542/3335 Berlin Philharmonic
		DG Priv 2543/3343 533
		Phillips 9500 399/7300 612 London Philharmonic
Tchaikovsky	*Swan Lake*	
	The Sleeping Beauty	*Famous Waltzes* Decca 410 292-4 Vienna Philharmonic
	The Nutcracker	Decca 410 551-2
	Eugene Onegin	CBS 650115/40 New York Philharmonic, Bernstein
	Capriccio italien	Phillips Sey 6527/7311 079 London Philharmonic, Stokowski
	Marche Slav	Decca Jub JB/KJBC 133
Verdi	*Triumphal March* from *Aida*	*Favorites of the Philharmonic* London Philharmonic Orchestra MFP MFP/TC MFP 1001
	Dance of the Moors, from *Aida*	HMV ASD/TC ASD 3983
	The Four Seasons	RCA Conifer 26.35036
	Macbeth	GD 2709 062/3371 022
	Otello	Decca SET 632
	Il Trovatore	RCA LSC 6194
Weber	*Invitation to the Dance*	*Famous Waltzes* Phillips Dig 514/7337 067
Ziehrer	Waltzes	Phillips Dig 6514/7337 068 & 069 (Vol. 1 and 2) Vienna Philharmonic

Bibliography

Bruno, H.J. *Riding in Formation.* Ruschlikon, West Germany: Albert Muller, 1976.

Bürkner, F. *The Life of a Rider.* Hildesheim, Germany: Olms, 1979.

Federal Ministry for Agriculture and Forestry, ed., *The Spanish Riding School in Vienna.* West Germany, 1965.

German Sport Association. *Sports.* West Germany, 1982.

Hanke, Christian-M. *The Book of the Quadrille.* Dusseldorf, West Germany: Sankt Georg, 1980.

Jacobs, Rita. *Music Therapy.* Bad Liebenzell, West Germany: Association for an Expanded Perception of Medical Practice, 1983.

"Newsletter for Horse Lovers." Dortmund, West Germany: Bibliophile Pocketbooks, Harenburg Communications, 1977.

Renner, H. *A Guide to Opera and Operetta.* Berchtesgarden, West Germany: Four Falkons Press, 1964.

Schnoor, H. *A History of Music.* Hamburg, West Germany: German Literary Press, 1973.

Seunig, Waldemar. *From Corral to Capriole: The Training of the Riding Horse.* Frankfurt, West Germany: Wolfgang Kruger, 1980.

Index

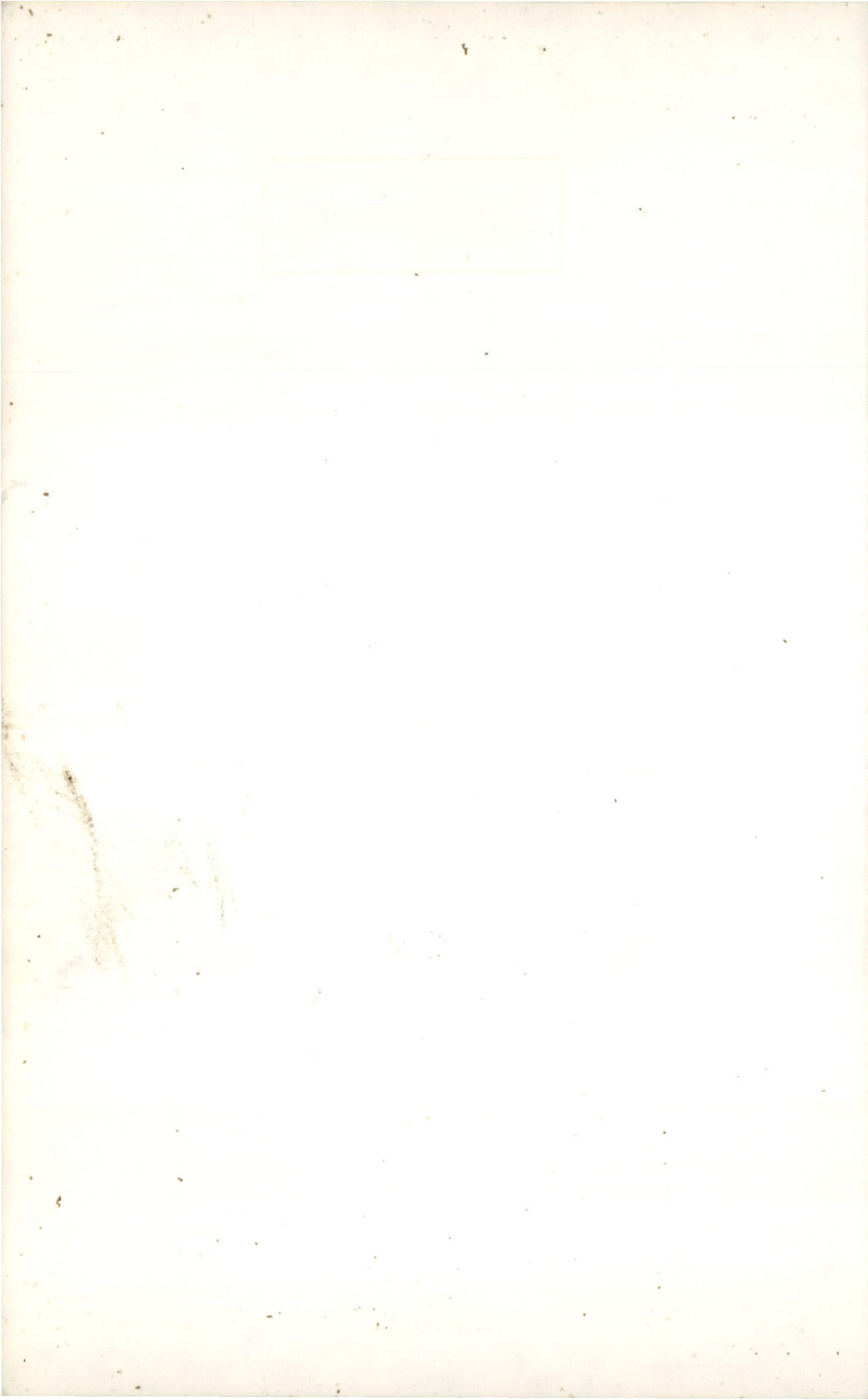